CONSERVATION
URBAN HABITATS

By Susan Carr and Andrew Lane

The Open University in association with the
Nature Conservancy Council

Hodder & Stoughton
LONDON SYDNEY AUCKLAND

Practical
CONSERVATION

Open University Course Team

Andrew Lane (Course Team Chair)

Susan Carr (Lecturer)

Graham Turner (BBC Producer)

Jennie Moffatt (Course Co-ordinator)

Amanda Smith (Editor)

Lesley Passey (Designer)

Keith Howard (Graphic Artist)

Roy Lawrance (Graphic Artist)

Jeff Edwards (Cartographer)

Julie Mortimer (Secretary)

ISBN 0 340 53369 2

First published 1993

Edited, designed and typeset by The Open University

Printed in the United Kingdom for the educational division of Hodder and Stoughton Ltd, Mill Road, Dunton Green, Sevenoaks, Kent by Butler & Tanner Ltd, Frome and London

Contents

This book is produced by The Open University as part of the *Practical Conservation* training programme which deals with all aspects of conservation on land that is managed largely for commercial or recreational purposes (see Figure 0.1).

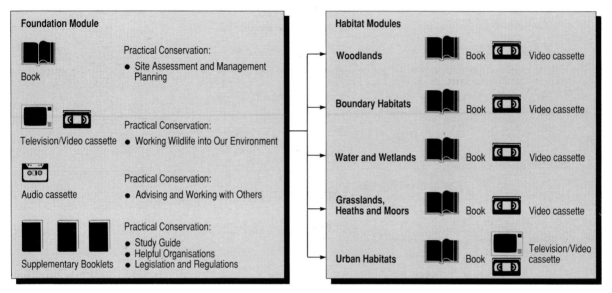

Figure 0.1
The Open University
teaching programme for
Practical Conservation

The foundation module covers site assessment and land use management planning in general and includes:

▶ the foundation book;

▶ a video cassette of a 50 minute television programme;

▶ a 60 minute audio cassette;

▶ two supplementary booklets;

▶ a *Study Guide* to the full programme.

This book with its accompanying 30 minute video cassette forms one of a series of modules on practical aspects of conservation management for a range of habitats:

▶ Woodlands;

▶ Boundary Habitats;

▶ Water and Wetlands;

▶ Grasslands, Heaths and Moors;

▶ Urban Habitats.

These training materials are suitable for use by groups or by individuals, studying alone or in association with a formal course. For those who would like to gain practical experience or a qualification, The Open University training programme is being incorporated into courses offered by colleges, field centres and other training bodies.

For further information please write to: Learning Materials Sales Office, The Open University, PO Box 188, Walton Hall, Milton Keynes MK7 6DH.

Chapter 1
INTRODUCTION

Our towns and cities are surprisingly rich in wildlife. At first sight, shopping centres bustling with people, roads crowded with traffic, large housing estates and industrial developments seem to be the most inhospitable of surroundings, and yet kestrels nest on city buildings, foxes scavenge in urban rubbish and orchids flourish on derelict industrial land. In each town and city there is a characteristic and often unique mixture of wild and introduced species that reflects an area's history and culture in much the same way as its architecture does. This wealth of wildlife is all the more valuable because it is so easily accessible. We can study and enjoy it on our own doorstep at any time.

Much urban wildlife is characterised by its adaptability and resilience to disturbance. For these species, threats to their existence come not so much from the presence of people, but from a lack of appreciation of their worth. Commonplace plants tend to be dismissed as undesirable weeds and are usually replaced in new developments by paving, mown turf and displays of bedding plants, which have little value for wildlife. This type of formal landscaping has generally been considered the most appropriate form of management for open space in built-up areas, and the presence of wild areas where vegetation is allowed to develop naturally is often perceived as a sign of neglect.

Since the 1970s, however, a combination of factors has begun to bring about a shift in that view. As a reaction to what they saw as the soulless character of some built-up areas, some landscape architects began to explore a more informal and people-centred approach to the design of urban open space. In this they were influenced by ideas from The Netherlands, where it has long been a policy to design semi-wild areas into city landscapes, and by similar approaches adopted in Sweden, Germany, the USA and Japan. At the same time, an increasing emphasis on practical project work in the school curriculum led to a growing demand from teachers for readily accessible nature study areas for field work. In industrial cities, a decline in traditional industries left large areas of derelict land and redundant buildings at a time when there was limited money available for redevelopment. Meanwhile, budgetary constraints forced local authorities to explore less costly methods of maintaining the large areas of green open space under their control.

The result has been an increasing interest in informal landscaping that involves working with wildlife rather than attempting to eliminate it. Such an approach benefits people as well as wildlife, as illustrated by the newspaper article shown in Box 1.1 (overleaf). More than 80% of people in Great Britain live in urban areas and many are without easy or regular access to the countryside. Small areas of semi-wilderness in built-up areas allow city dwellers and townspeople the pleasure of following the changing seasons, and provide opportunities to study nature at first hand, which makes them particularly valuable as an educational resource for local schools. Children who regularly have the opportunity to experience the fun and excitement of nature at close quarters from an early age are usually fascinated by it, and their interest readily develops into a life-long respect and concern for wildlife and for the environment as a whole.

Box 1.1 Children see nature make comeback in urban setting

It is a sunny spring morning next to the Arsenal soccer stadium and the boys from St Aloysius are examining the trials of life. In a yellow plastic tray are sticklebacks, tadpoles, the odd mayfly larva, all newly plucked from a small pond. The boys from St Aloysius, teenagers in school blazers and flannels, stand round the pond and discuss herons.

What, says one, is a heron? His companion frowns and concentrates. A fish, he suggests. The first shakes his head, ponders. Silence falls.

For those with eyes to see, the three acres of greenery around them are alive with incident. A willow warbler skulks in the bushes, the first orange-tip butterflies have arrived. But this is the borough of Islington in north London, and nature is an uncertain quantity.

Islington is thought to be the most built-up residential area in Britain. Less than two per cent of it provides cover for wildlife, compared with 17 per cent in neighbouring Camden and 44 per cent in Richmond.

Much of its green space is in tiny one-acre or two-acre pocket parks, painstakingly assembled from derelict housing and industry over the last two decades. It has two "areas of deficiency", where green space is more than a kilometre away.

Yet in Gillespie Park, where the boys of St Aloysius debate herons, nature has staged a comeback. David Goode believes that if it can happen there, it can happen anywhere.

Dr Goode has headed the London Ecology Unit since it was set up by the Greater London Council in 1981. It is now financed largely by the London boroughs.

Over the last decade, he argues, a revolution in attitudes has occurred. Ten years ago there were "virtually no ecologists" in London's local government; now there are 65. The number of local nature reserves has risen from two to 30. Volunteering and wildlife groups have boomed, in London and other towns and cities.

"Maybe it's a bit idealistic but I believe there was a yearning for direct contact with the natural world, not just seeing it vicariously on television. There is an appalling level of ignorance about natural history amongst a lot of people who live in cities. Without these kinds of opportunities it will get worse," he said.

The unit has produced 19 handbooks on nature conservation in the capital. Many would argue that its latest, a 60-page guide to the wildlife of Islington, is the least likely. Yet Islington has produced sightings of muntjac deer. Spotted flycatchers breed there. Five years ago botanists discovered a new "supergrass" in the borough: a hybrid previously unknown to science.

Gillespie Park, three acres of man-made woodland and meadow, is a sign of that progress. In 1981 it was "totally blitzed", a disused and treeless coal siding.

Two years ago it provided the first British breeding site of the Mediterranean long-tailed blue butterfly. It has a resident fox and has recorded 86 species of bird, 22 of butterfly and eight of dragonfly – a richer wildlife habitat, Dr Goode said, than most of the big city parks.

(Source: *The Independent*, 26 May 1992)

Wild areas can provide more varied, interesting and natural surroundings, often with considerable savings in maintenance costs. They provide a restful and pleasing contrast to hard surfaces and mown grass, allowing space for informal recreation and the chance for a brief respite from the pace and stress of urban life. Trees and shrubs provide shade and shelter, screen unsightly areas, dampen noise and help absorb pollutants such as dust and sulphur dioxide. Informal landscaping of areas such as industrial estates, old building sites and waste ground can contribute to a general environmental improvement and help stimulate investment in an area. Informal areas offer opportunities for local people to become involved in their management, which can strengthen a sense of community and help make the neighbourhood a more friendly and desirable place in which to live.

TOURIST?—I LIVE HERE MATE!

This book describes how you can play an active part in ensuring that the wildlife heritage of your town or city is appreciated to the full and that the open spaces are managed to maximum effect.

1.1 Who should read this book

This book should be of general interest to all those who live or work in towns and cities, but it is intended particularly for those who would like to play an active part in improving the wildlife value of their surroundings. Individual readers with a personal interest in wildlife will learn what actions they can take on their own to encourage wildlife and will gain a better appreciation of how their efforts can contribute to an area-wide strategy for nature conservation. Members of local groups, such as residents' associations, youth groups, pressure groups and natural history societies, will learn how they can influence the management of open space in their area, and participate in management projects or adopt a site to manage themselves. Those with a professional remit which encompasses urban land management, such as local authority councillors and officers, park superintendents, landscape architects, surveyors, civil engineers, employers and employees in commercial companies, and developers, will learn how they can adapt their management to take wildlife considerations into account, and how they can work with community groups to improve the local environment. The book should also be a valuable source of environmentally-based project work for teachers and their students in schools, colleges and universities.

1.2   How this book is structured

As with the other books in the *Practical Conservation* series, the overall emphasis here is on a systematic approach to wildlife conservation through the development of site-based management plans. In addition, this book encourages you to think of the management plan for a single site within the broader framework of a nature conservation strategy for a town or city as a whole. Even though you may not intend to take part in the management of a site yourself, it can be useful to know what is involved so that you can understand and influence what is done.

The production of a management plan is particularly valuable when the management of a site depends on the co-operation and involvement of several people, as is usually the case in urban areas, since it helps to provide a unified approach and to ensure continuity of management. The key stages in the development and implementation of a conservation management plan are described in detail in the foundation book, *Site Assessment and Management Planning*. In summary they involve:

1   assessing a site for its existing landscape and wildlife values, and its use by people;

2   identifying the objectives for and constraints to managing the site;

3   exploring the range of management options available and choosing amongst them;

4   incorporating the chosen options into a formal plan of action;

5   implementing the plan and monitoring its progress.

If you have read the other books in the *Practical Conservation* series, which are concerned mainly with rural habitats, you will already be familiar with the basic structure, in which successive chapters are devoted to stages in the development of a site management plan. This book follows a broadly similar pattern but includes a preliminary chapter describing how you as an individual can have a say in the management of open space in your area and a concluding chapter on the use of urban sites to encourage a wider public interest in wildlife and the environment.

Chapter 2 begins by describing some of the activities you can undertake on your own to encourage wildlife, and goes on to discuss how much more can be achieved by working in partnership with other people. It details the key role that local authorities can play in encouraging urban nature conservation, and explains the importance of adopting an area-wide strategy for nature conservation.

Chapter 3 describes the factors that contribute to the distinctive nature of urban wildlife sites and how to assess a site's value for wildlife. Chapter 4 discusses the assessment of sites for their value to the community.

Chapter 5 describes some of the management options available for maintaining and improving the value of existing wildlife habitats, while Chapter 6 looks at the opportunities and options for creating new habitats. The concluding chapter, Chapter 7, suggests ways of using and promoting urban wildlife sites to gain greater public recognition of the value of wildlife conservation in both urban and rural areas.

Since this book is intended to be a practical guide, you are encouraged to develop your own management plan for a piece of land to which you have legitimate access as you work through the chapters. Throughout the book there are exercises printed on a green background that are designed to help you to do this. Case study examples are provided at the end of most chapters to illustrate the points being made and to give you further guidance.

If your main interest is in caring for a particular wildlife feature, such as a garden pond, rather than in the management of a whole site, you should be able to find the relevant sections of the book by referring to the index, or to the sub-headings and margin notes, once you are familiar with the book's overall structure.

There is a video cassette which is designed to complement the information in this book. A video cassette symbol appears in the margin wherever a topic is illustrated on the video cassette. The contents of the video cassette are summarised in Box 1.2. You may find it useful to refer to other books in the *Practical Conservation* series if you would like more detailed information on management planning or specific wildlife habitat types, although they are not essential to an understanding of this book. If you would like to go more deeply into particular aspects of nature conservation in urban areas, such as urban ecology, there are several other excellent books that can be recommended for further reading and they are listed in Appendix I. Appendix II contains a glossary of terms for reference; each of the glossary entries is printed in bold type the first time that it appears in the text. Plants and animals are referred to by their common names (if they have one) for ease of reading, but their scientific (Latin) names are given in Appendix III.

Box 1.2 The video cassette – Working wildlife into our urban environment

The video cassette takes viewers on an urban wildlife safari by canal barge through the heart of the Black Country, in the West Midlands of England. A series of stops along the route illustrates the kind of wildlife sites that can be found in many old industrial areas and shows what can be done to encourage wildlife in new developments.

Stop 1 – Saltwell's Nature Reserve, including Doulton's clay pit. This is an area of mature woodland, which has been mined in the past for its coal, clay and sandstone. The warden, Tony Post, explains his role in discouraging fly-tipping and motorcycling so that local people and school groups can enjoy the site.

Stop 2 – a recently abandoned industrial site near Wolverhampton. Oliver Gilbert, an urban ecologist, shows the great variety of wild and cultivated plants that soon invade temporarily vacant plots of land.

Stop 3 – the Merry Hill development of shops and offices, showing the type of site where opportunities exist for creating new wildlife habitats.

Stop 4 – housing estates and a prize-winning wildlife garden, illustrating measures that every householder can take to encourage wildlife in gardens.

Stop 5 – Fens Pools, a wild open area surrounded by houses and industrial premises. This sequence illustrates the fun that local children have exploring the wildlife in one of the pools, and the dedicated and enthusiastic efforts of the local wildlife group in surveying the site, campaigning for recognition of its wildlife value by the local authority, and raising funds to manage it. The warden, Alec Connah, explains his role in acting as a focal point for those who use the site, and Sue Timms, the conservation officer for the local authority, describes how important members of the wildlife group were in securing recognition of the site's value for wildlife and for the community.

1.3 Urban open space sites, their origin and their wildlife potential

This section introduces the wide range of urban open space sites and features with wildlife potential, by grouping them according to how they have developed.

Towns and cities are constantly undergoing change. New areas are developed on the outskirts of existing built-up areas, old areas decay or fall into disuse and may subsequently be redeveloped. These cycles of development, illustrated by the example of Sheffield described in Box 1.3, result in the occurrence of four distinctive types of urban open space:

1   remnants of semi-natural countryside, such as old woodland, heathland and river valleys;

2   remnants of farmland with features such as hedges, ditches, copses and meadows;

3   designed open space, such as parks, sports fields, gardens, allotments and land associated with schools, hospitals, cemeteries and sewage works;

4   disused land, such as derelict industrial land, demolition sites and other disturbed waste ground.

Box 1.3   The development of Sheffield and its open space

On a map dating from 1771, Sheffield is shown as a small town, less than one square mile in extent, surrounded by hamlets. The economy of the area was based on agriculture and metal working, which used locally available ironstone, coal and charcoal and water power from the streams in the steep river valleys.

The opening of canal and rail links in the nineteenth century led to improved trade and the development of a huge steel and engineering industry in the town. Between 1800 and 1900 the population grew from 31,000 to 409,000. The water meadows of the River Don were covered by factories, dense areas of housing were built for the workers and the small hamlets were rapidly enveloped by the town. The wealth created was used to build large Victorian suburbs in the south-west of the city, up-wind of the works.

The large works and cramped workers' housing led to pollution and public health problems, including a cholera epidemic. Eventually new areas of housing were constructed, mainly in the south-west, and the coming of trams allowed further expansion of the suburbs. Inter-war slum clearance moved people into large municipal housing schemes on former farmland to the north and south-east, with parks and open space provided around schools and other public buildings. Post-war clearance of slums and bomb-damaged sites led to rehousing in tower blocks and more housing estates.

A booming industry and continuing high employment in the 1960s and 1970s encouraged further housing development on green field sites.

The sudden collapse of the steel industry in the early 1980s resulted in vast tracts of rubble, contaminated land and empty buildings. As in other cities where traditional industries are in decline, this decay brought home to the city council the need for environmental improvement and encouraged a 'green' approach to redevelopment.

Sheffield now covers about 363 square kilometres but is lucky in that even in the inner city almost one-third of the area is open space, as shown in Figure 1.1. Because it is a city built on hills, the steepness of the sandstone escarpments and the unstable nature of the shales has restricted building development. Many of the valley sides were left wooded for fuel production and some of these woods have survived or become acid grassland after felling. Other large areas have been left as amenity space amongst the large inter-war housing schemes built on farmland, particularly in the north and south-east. In the industrial zone there are large areas of recently derelict land or land that has been used for tipping. Further areas of vacant ground have been trapped between railway, canal and roads. The area of Victorian housing in the south-west is rich in mature gardens and street trees, with some older public parks and cemeteries. Mature gardens and allotments together constitute 22% of the inner city area.
(Source: Wild and Gilbert, 1988)

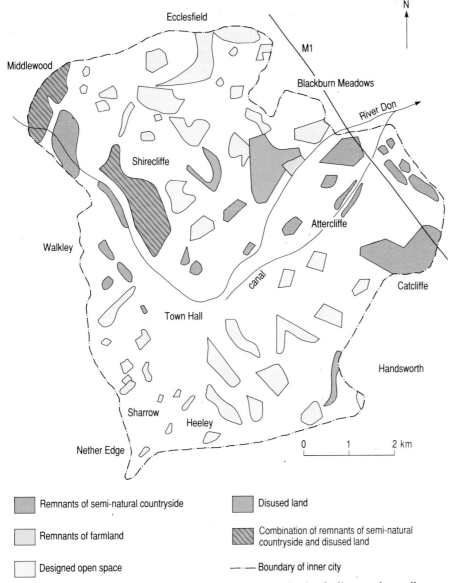

Figure 1.1 *Sheffield: areas of open space in the inner city (excluding gardens, allotments and areas less than 0.5 ha)*

Remnants of semi-natural countryside and farmland become trapped within built-up areas as urban development spreads, and are often described as **encapsulated countryside**. More extensive areas of farmland may remain at the margins of built-up areas, where they may be kept in reserve by the local authority for future development or deliberately preserved by planning policy, for example as **green belt** land, to contain urban sprawl and to keep adjacent settlements separate.

Designed open space includes all the areas that are deliberately designed into building developments, such as playing fields and grass surrounds to housing estates. A large proportion of this land has a uniform grass cover that is regularly mown and is of limited wildlife interest. However, appearances may be deceptive, especially in the case of long-established areas, which may have been derived directly from rural landscapes. For example, in Leicester a poorly

11

drained football pitch was found to contain a variety of flowers typical of an old meadow, such as great burnet, alpine lady's mantle and devil's bit scabious, which had survived despite regular heavy trampling. Part of a regularly mown and well-used bank in a Sheffield park was found to contain mat-grass, heath grass and harebell, all species derived from the former Crookesmoor after which the district is named. In parts of Birmingham former farmland hedges now surround gardens.

Disused land includes areas that have previously been developed, but that have fallen into disuse. Usually they are earmarked for redevelopment at some future date, but they may be left unmanaged for long enough to develop considerable wildlife interest.

A checklist of urban open space sites, grouped according to these four categories, is shown in Table 1.1, which also includes isolated features with value for wildlife, such as street trees and vegetated walls.

Table 1.1 Checklist of urban open space sites, grouped according to their origin

1 Remnants of semi-natural countryside

Old woodland	Chalk downland	Bog
Heathland	Marshland	Saltmarsh

(plus linear features such as rivers and streams, and coastal features such as sand dunes, shingle, cliffs)

2 Remnants of farmland

Arable fields	Copses
Pasture	Ponds

(plus linear features such as hedges and ditches)

3 Designed open space and land associated with urban services

Parks	Grassed areas around housing estates and landscaped surrounds of commercial and industrial premises	Churchyards
Public and private gardens		Cemeteries
Squares		Crematoria
Grounds of large old houses and institutions		Sewage works
Reservoirs	Allotments	
	Playing fields	
	Golf courses	

(plus linear features such as roadside verges, railway embankments and cuttings, canal banks, avenues of trees, and small isolated features such as street trees and vegetation-clad walls)

4 Disused land

Demolition sites	Quarries	Reclaimed refuse dumps
Spoil heaps	Redundant dockland	Waste ground trapped by road and housing developments
Pits	Disused railway land	
		Neglected cemeteries and abandoned allotments and gardens

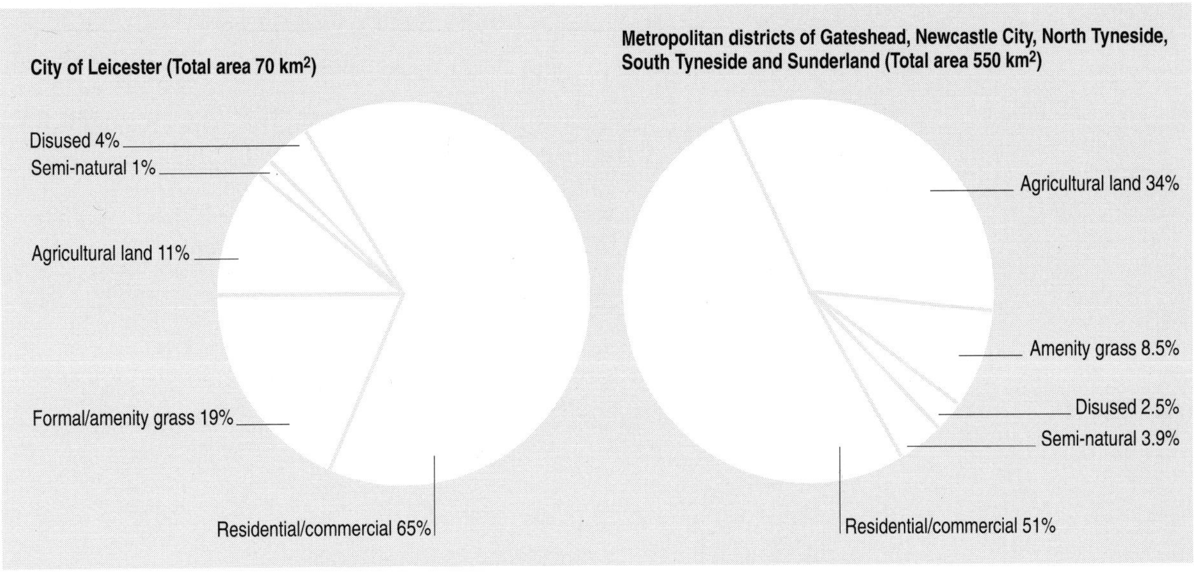

City of Leicester (Total area 70 km²)

Metropolitan districts of Gateshead, Newcastle City, North Tyneside, South Tyneside and Sunderland (Total area 550 km²)

Disused 4%
Semi-natural 1%

Agricultural land 11%

Formal/amenity grass 19%

Residential/commercial 65%

Agricultural land 34%

Amenity grass 8.5%

Disused 2.5%
Semi-natural 3.9%

Residential/commercial 51%

Figure 1.2   Land use in two urban areas. (Sources: Leicester City Council, 1989; Nature Conservancy Council, 1988)

No two towns or cities are alike in their development, so that the proportion of land that falls into each of the four categories varies considerably from place to place. Since there is some overlap between the categories and local authorities differ in the way in which they categorise their open space, direct comparisons between different urban areas are difficult, but Figure 1.2 indicates the extent of different categories of urban land use in Leicester and in Tyne and Wear as examples.

The type and variety of wildlife which a site supports depends not only on its origin and physical factors such as soil and climate, but on its age and permanence, past and present management, type and intensity of use, extent of pollution and disturbance, and sources of introduction of new species. The effects of all these factors are discussed in Chapter 3.

The social value of a site with wildlife potential is affected by factors such as the accessibility of the site to the community, its aesthetic appeal, and its cultural and historical significance, as discussed in Chapter 4.

To help you begin to identify the variety of sites that may have wildlife potential in your own area, the next section provides a simple exercise for you to do. At the end of the chapter there are two case study examples showing the results of a similar exercise done in Reading and Dundee.

1.4   Exercise 1: Identifying wildlife areas near you

This exercise is designed to raise your awareness of the areas with wildlife potential that exist in your immediate surroundings (or to draw your attention to the lack of such areas). You are not expected to go to great lengths to supply missing information. Simply record what you already know, can easily observe or readily find out. A systematic approach to surveying and assessing urban open space will be described in subsequent chapters.

Using the checklist shown in Table 1.1 as a guide:

1   List, or indicate on a map, all the areas of open space within a distance of half a kilometre from your home, workplace or school. (If you live in a rural area, do the exercise for a built-up area you know well.) Be guided by the time you have available and the abundance of open space in your area in deciding how comprehensive to be; for example, in deciding whether or not to include very small sites, isolated features and the space occupied by private gardens.

  Use a map with a scale of 1:25,000 or less to help identify the area concerned and any open space hidden from public view. See Box 1.4 if you need further guidance on the type of map to use and the appropriate scale.

2   As far as possible, categorise sites according to their origin with the help of the checklist in Table 1.1. Use more than one category for a site if relevant.

3   If known, note for each site whether it is publicly or privately owned and whether or not there is public access.

Box 1.4   Choice of map and scale

The scale of a map is usually expressed as a ratio, for example 1:25,000. At this scale, 1 metre on paper represents 25,000 metres on the ground, or, to express it in more practical units, 1 centimetre on paper represents 0.25 km (one-quarter of a kilometre) on the ground.

The most appropriate type and scale of map depends on your purpose and the size of the area in which you are interested. Ordnance Survey maps, or leisure maps based on them, show areas of vegetation such as parks and woods. If you are interested in identifying open areas throughout the built-up area of your town or city, maps at a scale of 1:25,000 (usually available 'off the shelf') or, even better, 1:10,000 (may need to be ordered) are appropriate.

For assessing the vegetation and planning the management of a particular site, a more detailed map, at a scale of 1:2500 or even 1:1250, may be needed. Your local authority may be able to help you obtain copies of these if you explain your purpose.

Street maps are useful for locating the exact position of sites on the ground. The yellow pages of the telephone directory contain street maps of town and city centres at a scale of 1:20,000. More detailed street maps with a wider coverage are usually available from newsagents and bookshops locally.

Since the area of open space in urban areas is constantly changing, it is important to use up-to-date maps or at least to be aware that old maps may be inaccurate and need checking.

1.5   Case study examples

Reading

Areas of open space within a distance of 0.5 kilometre from a home in Caversham are shown in Figure 1.3 and listed in the key below it. There is little derelict land in this area as land values are very high.

Figure 1.3   Areas of open space within 0.5 kilometre of a home in Caversham, Reading

Remnant of semi-natural countryside

1   Southern edge only of small area of beech/oak ancient woodland. Owned by Reading Borough Council. With public access.

Remnant of farmland

2   Grass field mown for hay annually, with invading scrub from surrounding hedgerows. Ownership unknown. Public footpath and informal access.

Designed open space and land associated with urban services

3   Allotment gardens. Owned by Reading Borough Council. Access to cardholders only.

4   Primary school playing field. Owned by Berkshire County Council. No public access.

5   Private school playing field with row of lime trees. Assumed to be owned by trustees. No public access.

6   Wooded grounds and parkland of large house. Recently sold for housing development. Public access as roads are developed.

7   Parkland with planted trees and remnants of old field hedgerows. Owned by Reading Borough Council. Public access at all times.

8   Mown grass around flats. Owned by Reading Borough Council. Preferred access for tenants, but open.

9   Steep embankment to road with dense elm scrub. Assumed to be owned by Berkshire County Council. Unfenced but very steep.

10   Victorian cemetery with many evergreen trees, mown only once a year, and rich in wildlife. Owned by Reading Borough Council. Public access at restricted times.

Disused land

11   Derelict allotment gardens with bramble invasion on steeper slopes. Owned by Reading Borough Council. Access to cardholders only.

(Source: Linda Carter, Reading Urban Wildlife Group)

Dundee

Areas of open space, including private gardens, within a 0.5 kilometre radius of a spot in inner Dundee are shown in Figure 1.4. This area is typical of the inner city, with tenements, council housing, derelict land and private housing with gardens. Most of the public open space is landscaping around housing schemes and industrial premises. Two of the derelict areas have been colonised over the past 10 years by scrub and rank grassland.

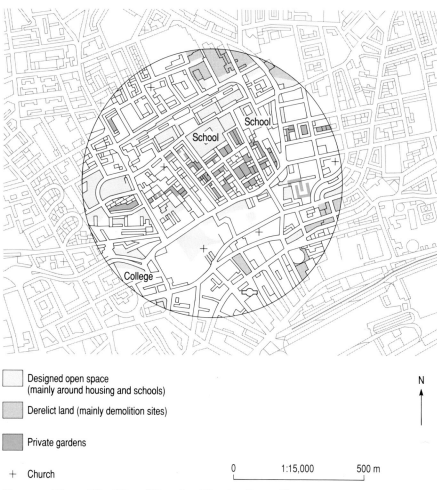

Designed open space
(mainly around housing and schools)

Derelict land (mainly demolition sites)

Private gardens

+   Church

0   1:15,000   500 m

N

Figure 1.4   Areas of open space within 0.5 kilometre of a spot in inner Dundee

(Source: Alison Silk, City of Dundee District Council)

Chapter 2

WORKING ALONE AND TOGETHER

To become actively involved in practical conservation you need to have some sense of purpose. Listing or marking on a map all the familiar open space sites and features nearby may increase your awareness of their existence but does not necessarily suggest why you should take any action. Unless you already have a specific project in mind, you need to reflect for a while about your own interests in relation to these open areas and about what you like and dislike about them. Table 2.1 (overleaf) shows the results of a survey of visitors to three parks developed as wildlife areas: Gillespie Road Park in the London Borough of Islington, Newbridge Farm Recreation Ground in Birmingham and Birchwood Brook Park in Warrington New Town. Check whether or not any of their opinions correspond with your views about your own area.

Thinking about local wildlife features and sites in these terms should prompt ideas about how you would like them to be managed. If you enjoy them as they are, you may want to ensure that the existing form of management continues and that no undesirable changes take place. If there are aspects that you dislike you may be keen to see improvements. If you feel that you and your community are deprived of access to wildlife and natural surroundings you may want to find ways of changing this situation. In all cases you need to take action if you are to achieve the type of surroundings you want.

Initially you may feel that there is little you can do, apart from taking steps to encourage wildlife in your own garden if you have one. Even this action alone can have tremendous benefits for wildlife if other people do likewise, given the large proportion of urban land usually occupied by private gardens. However, you do not have to limit your actions to land that you own or control.

You can record the wildlife on any site to which you have access, monitor planning applications and site development, express your own views on how a site could be managed by contacting the owner or the local authority, participate in public consultations on local planning policy, and lobby for wildlife to be considered in development by writing to the press, your local government representative, Member of Parliament (MP) or Member of the European Parliament (MEP).

All these activities will be more effective, and usually more enjoyable too, if they are undertaken as part of a group rather than working alone. Your opinions about a site's management are more likely to influence people in positions of power if you can show that other people share your view. As a group, you will be able to share skills, knowledge and effort, and you will probably have better access to resources. You may be able to draw on the support of local businesses, and, if the group is part of a national network, obtain additional expertise and back-up when needed. Together, you could take on the management of a local wildlife site.

In all activities to do with urban wildlife conservation local authorities can play a key enabling role. They often own, or are responsible for, the management of a large proportion of urban land. Through planning

Table 2.1 The likes and dislikes of visitors to three urban natural parks (a total of 180 people were surveyed)

Likes	Percentage of visitors	Dislikes	Percentage of visitors
Peace and quiet	21	No dislikes	36
Naturalness/countryside feel	18	Litter/dumping	15.5
Openness	16	Too many dogs/complaint about dogs	15
Trees	13.5	Vandalism	12
Nature/wildlife	12	Uncared-for appearance	8.5
Convenient	10	Feel insecure	6
Pond/river/brook	10	Children causing nuisance	4.5
Good for children	7	Teenage gangs	3.5
Flowers	5.5	Not enough facilities	3.5
Good for walking the dog	5.5	Feel exposed	3
Scenery	5.5	Nowhere to sit/no seats	3
Seats	4.5	Too small/narrow	3
Relaxing	4	Not enough people	2.5
Good for walking	4	Cycles/motorbikes	2.5
Well maintained	3	Run down/needs more money	2.5
Landscape plan/layout	1.5	No one to explain things	2.5
Few dogs/dog-free area	1.5	Don't know what/nothing to do	2
No traffic	1.5	Danger from pond/river/brook	2
Good for sports/games	1.5	No park keeper/not enough rangers	2
Less vandalism/nothing for vandals	1	Brook/artificiality/pollution	2
Fresh air	1	Poor condition of paths	1.5
Sunset	1	Gypsies	1
Meeting people/having a chat	0.5	Flies/mosquitoes	1
Good for hide-and-seek	0.5	Encroachment of houses	1
Winding path	0.5	Too near railway	1
Off the beaten track	0.5	Way people treat park	1
Tree nursery	0.5	Too many people	0.5
Green	0.5	Gravel path not very natural	0.5
Fresh looking	0.5	Broken glass	0.5
Looking at different things	0.5	No signs	0.5
No sports	0.5	Lack of colours/flowers	0.5

(Source: Millward and Mostyn, 1989)

procedures they can influence private landowners. They can provide information, advice, expertise and resources for voluntary groups who would like to be involved in managing local sites themselves. Although not all of them are yet equally sympathetic to nature conservation issues, local authorities exist to serve the needs of the community, so it is up to you to find out what powers they have and to let them know how they can best fulfil their role.

Many of the activities described in this book can be undertaken by people working alone and can be applied to private gardens and small isolated features, but the main emphasis is on working in partnership with others to improve the nature conservation and recreational value of publicly accessible sites. This chapter describes some of the main conservation groups that exist, how to form your own group if necessary, and how to secure resources for environmental projects. It summarises the part that local authorities can play in supporting urban nature conservation, and discusses the mechanisms for promoting liaison between different organisations and groups. A practical exercise and two case study examples of community groups complete the chapter.

2.1   Joining an existing group

Setting up a new group requires a considerable commitment in terms of time and energy, so before contemplating this step you need to find out what local groups already exist. There may be existing groups that cater for your interests and that share your aims, or that could be persuaded to adopt your cause, or some of whose members might be interested in forming the nucleus of a new group. Local libraries can usually supply information about all groups in the area, and the planning department of the local authority often has a list of voluntary groups and organisations which they routinely inform or consult on environmental matters. The supplementary booklet *Helpful Organisations*, which accompanies the foundation book to this series, provides information about most of the principal nature conservation organisations. The Environmental Unit of the National Council for Voluntary Organisations can supply details of local networks of community groups.

National groups

On a national basis, the groups whose members are most closely involved in the management of urban wildlife sites are those linked together through the Urban Wildlife Partnership, which is linked to and supported by the Royal Society for Nature Conservation (RSNC) Wildlife Trusts Partnership. They include the urban wildlife trusts (such as the London Wildlife Trust), urban wildlife groups (such as those in Reading, Sheffield, Plymouth and Swansea), and a variety of urban-based wildlife projects, usually set up by local authorities (such as the Derby City Wildlife Project and the Eastbourne Wildlife Project).

Wildlife trusts and groups undertake a wide range of activities, including conducting wildlife surveys, preparing site management plans, carrying out practical conservation tasks, providing information and educational material, and advising smaller community-based groups. They sometimes purchase, rent, or operate management agreements with the owners of key wildlife sites to safeguard sites from development.

Other nation-wide groups with a practical involvement in conservation are the local groups of the British Trust for Conservation Volunteers (BTCV) and its equivalent in Scotland, the Scottish Conservation Projects (SCP). BTCV and SCP own no sites of their own, but their members carry out conservation tasks, such as clearing ponds and scrub, on sites that are owned and managed by others. BTCV and SCP also run extensive practical training programmes and loan out equipment to local community groups. They can advise community groups about obtaining insurance cover.

Some national organisations become involved in urban wildlife sites from time to time and for a specific purpose; for example, members of Women's Institutes have surveyed the wildlife of churchyards country-wide, including those in towns and cities; the British Trust for Ornithology (BTO) regularly organises surveys of the populations and distribution of birds; WATCH, an environmental club for young people run by the RSNC, has conducted a nation-wide survey of nature in towns with the help of school groups; local groups of national conservation organisations such as the Royal Society for the Protection of Birds (RSPB) or Friends of the Earth (FoE) sometimes support campaigns to save threatened urban wildlife sites in their area. In some places the National Trust runs local volunteer groups, and the Woodland Trust sometimes acquires and manages woodland in urban areas and runs local events.

Local and community groups

There are many local groups that are associated with a particular urban site; some examples are described in Box 2.1. Sometimes people work together to encourage wildlife in a communal area in whose management they already have some say, for example their school grounds, churchyard or workplace, as in the case of the staff at Perkins Technology in Peterborough. Often, though, the trigger for the formation of a group is a threat to develop a wild area or green space that local people do not own or control but that they have come to regard as an important part of their surroundings. These groups take many different forms and vary considerably in their functions. In some cases, the group is simply a loose (and often temporary) association of residents who lobby the local authority with their views, as in the case of the Royate Hill Embankment Action Group in Bristol. In others, the group is actively involved with the management of a site, as in the case of the Sunnyside Community Gardens in Islington, London.

2.2 Setting up a new group

If you find that no existing group fulfils your purpose and decide to form your own group, you should discuss your ideas with as many people as possible first. Talk with the leaders of other local groups to find out their aims and objectives, both to avoid duplication of effort and to seek their support and collaboration. Groups such as local preservation societies, natural history societies and archaeological societies are likely to be useful contacts. Community-based groups such as residents' associations and parent–teacher associations may be interested if your ideas concern open space in their immediate area. Inform local authority officers of your plans, since they also may be able to provide help and information. Most important of all, ensure that there are others who share your objectives and are prepared to take an active part in establishing and running the group.

Initial meeting

Publicise your proposal to form a group by holding an open meeting. Before the meeting, agree broad aims and objectives for the group with key supporters as a basis for discussion at the meeting. Arranging a guest speaker or some other attraction can help tempt people to attend. Give some thought to the groups of people you hope to involve, since this can help

Box 2.1 Examples of local groups

Staff at Perkins Technology

With the support of their company bosses, staff at Perkins Technology have transformed their one acre site on an industrial estate in Peterborough into an oasis for wildlife. The leader of the project, the company's standards controller, took a crash-course in wildlife habitat creation, seeking advice from the Peterborough Wildlife Group, and imparting the knowledge acquired to the rest of the group.

As a result, the site now boasts a spinney, a dry-stone wall, a wildflower meadow, various heaps of dead wood and compost, shrub banks, humps and hollows, and a 55,000 litre pond (filled by the company fire brigade in less than an hour). Employees brought in buckets of mud from their own ponds to introduce bugs, beetles and other creatures into the pond. The staff's children helped plant the hedge.

Some of the more exciting wildlife visitors to the site include mammals such as a weasel, bats, muntjac deer and numerous short-tailed voles, which appear to have taken control of one of the sandy banks, much to the enjoyment of the design and research staff whose office windows overlook the site.

(Source: *Urban Wildlife News,* Vol. 8, No. 3, August 1991)

Royate Hill Embankment Action Group

This group set itself up as a direct result of a threat to remove and build on Royate Hill Embankment in Bristol. This railway embankment, with its mixture of attractive grassland and scrub habitats, provides a popular and very visible wild space in an otherwise built-up area of the city.

Working with Avon Wildlife Trust, the group got together when the development proposals went to public enquiry in July 1991. They organised a petition, collecting over 1000 signatures from people living nearby, and sent leaflets to local people to encourage them to write to the planning inspector. Many people responded, writing in and making regular appearances at the 13-day public inquiry. The group read their own proof of evidence. As a result, the inspector turned down the development, saying in his report:

'From the many letters received and the attendance and representations made at the inquiry, I am in no doubt that residents derive much pleasure from the changing seasonal colours and variety of vegetation on the sites and from the wildlife they support. ...the fact that there is no formal access to the land does not in my opinion lower materially its visual and emotional value to those who live nearby, pass through or visit the area'.

(Postscript: subsequently, in May 1992, the landowners started to bulldoze the site, despite the inspector's decision. Even though the members of the local community were unable to prevent some damage being done they are still fighting to save the site. As a result of their efforts, Avon County Council have declared their intention to designate the site as a **Local Nature Reserve** (LNR) and to buy it by compulsory purchase.)

(Source: Helen Hall, Avon Wildlife Trust)

Sunnyside Community Gardens

Sunnyside Community Gardens is the name of a site and of the people who manage it. The site was previously a derelict rubbish dump on ground where 25 Victorian houses had been demolished and is surrounded by high density housing. When plans were announced to build a road across the site, the North Islington Housing Rights Group instead suggested that the area should be turned into a public open space, to be maintained and enjoyed by local people for gardening and recreation.

Now Sunnyside Gardens includes a wild space with a hedgerow, flowerbeds and shrubs, a herb bed, 14 garden plots, a comfrey bed (as a source of compost), compost bins and a large area of grass. Members of Sunnyside Gardens run the site with the help of three part-time workers, one of whom works with groups who have special needs and another with local schools. Financial support comes from Islington Council, the Education Authority and two charitable trusts. The group is currently fund-raising to install an ecology classroom on the site.

(Source: Paul Lipsham, Sunnyside Community Gardens)

guide the choice of venue and time. For example, the support of local parents might most easily be gained by holding a meeting in a local school immediately after school when they come to collect their children. If possible, talk to people beforehand to encourage them to participate, since many people are reluctant to attend and voice their opinions at meetings. Try to involve all members of the community, especially disadvantaged or minority groups who might not normally come forward. Older people and people who are disabled may be glad to help with record-keeping, deal with correspondence or sign petitions even though they may not be able to participate in physical tasks. People from minority ethnic groups may be a stimulating source of ideas drawn from their own traditions and culture, as described in Box 2.2.

Advertise the purpose of the meeting and its date, time and venue in public places such as libraries, community centres and shops, by informing the local press and radio station and by distributing leaflets to houses. Keep a written record of the meeting and collect names and addresses of those who would like to be involved or kept informed. Even if the number of people who decide to give the group their active support is small, a wider membership or community involvement can often be maintained by continuing to hold open meetings at intervals to keep people informed of the group's activities and to exchange views.

Structure

The extent to which a group requires a formal structure is likely to depend on its size and its aims. Unless the group is very loosely structured, it is usual to have at least three officers: a chair (to take the lead and to liaise with other organisations), a secretary (to keep records of meetings, deal with correspondence and help initiate activities), and a treasurer (to keep accurate records of financial transactions). It can be an advantage to the group if the chair is an influential or well-known member of the community. In larger groups, there may be other responsibilities that can be assigned to particular members, for example editing a newsletter, collecting membership fees, or gaining publicity for the group. If the group is to become actively involved in site management, there may need to be a steering committee, possibly involving representatives from other groups, to agree policy for the site, and/or working parties to participate in specific tasks. It is a good idea to share responsibilities as widely as possible, and to offer a range of activities requiring different skills, to maintain members' interest and commitment and to avoid overburdening a few.

The group should seek professional advice, for example from the National Council for Voluntary Organisations, other well-established groups, a local Citizens Advice Bureau or a solicitor, about legal matters such as drafting a formal constitution, applying for charitable status, arranging insurance cover and meeting legal obligations. To provide protection to the group, and to individual officers and members, a written constitution is advisable and insurance cover is essential.

2.3 Securing resources

Sooner or later your group is likely to need additional funds to finance its activities. You may need money to pay for a campaign, advice or publicity, or to buy tools and materials. If you want to attract visitors and school groups to a site, you may want funds for leaflets, signs, displays and a visitor centre. Whatever you plan to do, you need to think through the financial implications carefully.

Box 2.2 A cultural garden

A city's human inhabitants, like its flora and fauna, are international. Judy Ling Wong, Director of the Black Environment Network (BEN), strongly believes that all local environmental projects should encourage people to think about the international and global environment too. The garden described here is an example of the type of multi-cultural project that her network supports, through its Ethnic Minorities Award Scheme (EMAS).

In 1987, a Chinese dance company applied to EMAS for funding for a 'Far Eastern and African Plant Garden'. Their site for the garden was Walnut Tree Walk School, a multi-racial school in Kennington, south London. The dance company had been working with the school on a project called 'Storm and Rebirth' about the loss of the school's only tree in the storm of 1987. The dance portrayed the destructiveness of the storm; the garden symbolised the rebirth.

People's imagination and enthusiasm were caught by the idea of a cultural garden – a living, growing link through which the children could experience and truly 'touch' their countries of origin. Features of the garden include river pebble beds, a mound, a bamboo ring surrounding pure white gravel that can be raked into designs, and log seats and log features commemorating the storm.

Most of the plants, bought from the Royal Horticultural Society's Wisley Gardens, are from areas of the Far East, the same latitudes as England, so there are no problems growing them here at all. In fact, some are very common in British gardens, and having them in the Far Eastern garden has had the effect of local children coming back to school saying 'There are Chinese plants in my garden too!' The children can see the identified plants in the Far Eastern and African garden all around them in nearly every 'English' garden, showing that aspects of their origin have been here and been loved for a very long time.

The garden has azaleas, rhododendrons and maples from Northern and Central China, Korea and Japan; irises with relations right across the latitudes from Japan to the USA; columbines, Chinese mother of thousands, Japanese bleeding hearts, mountain peonies, Himalayan roses, bamboo, wisteria, jasmine, Chinese lanterns and camellias. African representatives in the garden include red hot pokers, stonecrops and ferns.

(Source: *Urban Wildlife News,* Vol. 8, No. 1, February 1991)

There are a number of sources of funds but there are also a great many people seeking funding, so you need a well thought out proposal to put to potential sponsors. Be clear what you need the money for, how much you need, when you will need it, and how you will supplement it if it is not enough. Spell out why you think your project is important, urgent, interesting or different, and the benefits it could bring to your sponsors, your supporters and the general public. If possible, provide evidence of other projects that you have successfully completed and letters of support from other organisations or local people.

The simplest way of raising funds is to seek them first from your members and supporters. They should need no convincing of the merits of your cause. Money can also be raised from the general public by organising such things as plant sales, car boot sales and special events. Local authorities can be a major source of funding, or at least of help in kind. Many have special budgets for community projects or for specific purposes such as tree planting, land clearance and public amenities.

Local businesses and commercial companies may be prepared to support community projects, especially if by doing so they get good publicity. They may provide equipment or services at reduced rates, or be prepared to advise your group on seeking other sources of funding. There may be useful contacts with local firms among your members.

Several national companies run award schemes and competitions for community projects. Current examples include the Shell Better Britain Campaign, the Kodak Conservation Awards and the Forte Community Chest. They are likely to have many applicants, so before applying it is worth investigating how many awards there are and what the criteria are for selection. Similar advice applies to applications for funds from the large number of charitable trusts, each of which may have their own conditions and procedures. A complete list is provided in the *Directory of Grant-Making Trusts*, which you should be able to consult in your public library. Other groups may be able to advise you on the trusts that are most likely to support your type of project.

Funds are also available for environmental projects from central government departments and from statutory bodies such as English Nature, the Countryside Commission, the Countryside Council for Wales and Scottish Natural Heritage. For some nature conservation projects, funds may be available from the Forestry Commission, the Woodland Trust or the Royal Society for Nature Conservation.

Whatever your source of funds, make sure your sponsors know their help is appreciated, keep them informed of progress and, if appropriate, invite them to special events. Advice from a variety of sources on getting help and co-operation is given in Box 2.3.

2.4   The role of the local authority

It is important for your group to be aware of the support that the local authority can provide for urban nature conservation, and to establish a good working relationship with local authority officers (the paid staff) and sympathetic councillors (the elected representatives). It is also useful to find out what land the local authority owns, as much of it may have scope for increased conservation.

Scope for local authority support

There are a great many ways in which local authorities can promote wildlife conservation in urban areas, as summarised in Table 2.2 (overleaf). Some authorities use their powers to the full, while others simply pay lip service to conservation but might be encouraged to do more if there was sufficient pressure from the local community. Some authorities, such as Leicester City Council, have a policy of encouraging participation by local people in the design and management of parks and open spaces, while others may be unwilling or unable to allow the involvement of volunteers, especially if it might affect agreements with unions.

 If you think that any of the powers listed in Table 2.2 might be used to help your group achieve its aims, contact local authority officers to seek their advice. They are the people most directly concerned with the day-to-day implementation of policy. If you feel that the local authority makes insufficient use of the powers that it has, a sympathetic councillor may be prepared to support your case and argue for a change in policy.

Box 2.3 Obtaining help and co-operation

Personnel from widely varying sectors of the community were asked for their advice to small community groups seeking help. These are their replies.

Linda Carter, Reading Urban Wildlife Group

When approaching other organisations for help, have a clear idea what your aims and objectives are. Give the impression of a confident, highly motivated group by the presentation of your case. Avoid being aggressive or an apologist. Gaining respect for your group usually reaps rewards.

Have a shopping list of ways in which other organisations can help you – offers come in cash and kind. It is often worth talking to likely organisations before sending a letter. That way you know what they have to offer. Send correspondence to named individuals and if necessary follow up your letter with a telephone call.

Maintain contact with other urban groups. There is a lot to learn from shared expertise and experience.

Barbara J Maher, Senior Planner, Reading Borough Council

Acquaint yourself with the workings of local government to fully appreciate legal and political constraints upon local authority officers. Be clear about your aims and objectives and assess these against the background of the above to be realistic about what you can achieve and timescales.

Be positive and helpful, not critical and derogatory.

Offer your services and become indispensable. Many local authorities have no in-house practical conservation expertise and will welcome your help and advice.

In this way your voice will be heard, your opinions respected and valued and you will be in the best position to obtain local authority grant aid – or to keep it when cuts are made.

Councillor Mark Drapes, Slough Corporation

Find out who your local councillors are by getting a list from the civic offices or library. Nature conservation may be the responsibility of parish, borough or county council or a combination of all three. Local councillors work voluntarily and do not always have time for letter writing. If your letter does not get a reply follow it up by phoning for your answer.

Councillors are publicity seekers. If you want help for your project invite a councillor along, take a photo of the councillor with your group and issue it as a press release to the local papers.

If you are having trouble communicating with council officers, phone your local councillor and seek advice on the best person to contact.

Communicate your philosophy and ideas to your councillor.

Freely offer your advice throughout the year, not just when consulted. In time your group will be recognised as an authority and your advice sought more often.

British Telecom

BT's Community Programme gives almost £15 million a year to community causes – but the money is never enough to meet the thousands of requests we receive.

A written approach is best as a first step. Confine your initial approach to a typed one-sheet letter of standard-sized A4 paper and then follow it up with a telephone call. Make your suggestion short and to the point but do promise a more detailed and structured proposal if your initial approach is favourably received.

Local authority structure

When contacting the local authority, it may not always be easy to find out who is responsible for what. It pays to be persistent, and to cultivate sympathetic contacts once established.

County or, in Scotland, regional councils currently decide on the overall land use policy framework but it is city, borough and, in small towns, district councils that are most closely involved with detailed policy about the use and development of urban land.

Table 2.2 Powers available to local authorities to help promote wildlife conservation in urban areas

Development control

Refusal of applications	Planning permission can be refused to protect nature areas.
Conditions on planning permission	In granting planning permission, conditions can prevent harmful effects (e.g. pollution, destruction of wildlife habitats) and/or ensure positive benefits (e.g. creation of new landscape features).
Development Agreements	Primarily restrictive tool which regulates the development or use of land. Can minimise harmful effects of development and lead to positive benefits (e.g. restoration of site after mineral extraction). Agreements can indicate details of restorative landscape design and they are frequently used to achieve landscaping outside the area of planning application. This can include the creation of a nature area. Agreements can protect a site of value against inimical changes and this is enforceable in perpetuity.
Enforcement Notices and Stop Notices	Used to stop development which is occurring without planning permission.

Acquisition of land

Acquisition by agreement	Power to acquire by agreement any land that is needed for development, redevelopment and improvement, or needed to achieve proper planning of an area. This includes the purchase of land to protect its nature conservation value or where nature conservation is one of several objectives for the land.
Compulsory purchase	Where it is not possible to purchase land by agreement. Appliable to land needed for development, redevelopment or improvement.

Land management

Management Agreements	Local authorities can enter into management agreements with owners and occupiers of land in town or country to regulate the use and management of land.
Bylaws	Bylaws for regulating use of land. Can create and enforce bylaws on nature reserves and other specified areas.
Derelict land	Grants available to local authorities from the Department of the Environment to fund reclamation and improvement of derelict land. Can be used to establish wildlife habitats, nature reserves, community gardens, etc. Grants payable for land acquisition, site surveys, reclamation works, administrative expenses, consultants' fees and removal of derelict buildings. Priority given to inner city areas.

Trees

Tree Preservation Orders (TPOs)	In the interests of amenity, to preserve individual trees, groups of trees, and woodlands through prohibiting cutting down, lopping, up-rooting, wilful damage or destruction. Also used to ensure replacement of existing trees and that new planting is retained.
Tree planting	Local authorities are empowered to plant trees and to carry out works for the purpose of reclaiming or improving derelict land or preparing it for re-use. They can plant on their own land or with the consent of all persons interested in the land. In addition land can be acquired compulsorily for the purpose of tree planting (included is the planting of bushes, the planting or sowing of flowers, the sowing of grasses or the laying of turf). Grant aid is available from the Forestry Commission, Countryside Commission, English Nature, Countryside Council for Wales, Scottish Natural Heritage, or Department of the Environment (as part of derelict land reclamation scheme).
Trees and planning permission	In granting planning permission, local authorities have a duty to ensure that adequate provision is made for the preservation and planting of trees, and to make TPOs as necessary. This includes protecting trees on, or beside, development sites, and providing land for planting.

26

Local Nature Reserves (LNRs)	Local authorities have the power to designate LNRs and create bylaws in respect of them. Bylaws can prohibit activities which damage the area. Grants may be available from English Nature, Countryside Council for Wales or Scottish Natural Heritage.
Country parks	Local authorities have powers to establish, maintain and manage country parks for public enjoyment. Land may be acquired by agreement or compulsion, or parks may be set up on land belonging to others by agreement with them.
Sites of Special Scientific Interest (SSSIs)	Local authorities can submit areas to English Nature, Countryside Council for Wales or Scottish Natural Heritage as candidates for notification as SSSIs. Notification offers some degree of control over land use changes and specifies any operations which would be likely to damage the flora, fauna or other features.

Definitive Maps	Local authorities must keep Definitive Maps and statements of public rights of way under review and prepare new maps for areas not previously surveyed. Useful for stimulating production of pamphlets and information boards illustrating guided walks.
Rights of way	Orders of agreements can be made for creating public footpaths across previously inaccessible land. Statutory duty to maintain public rights of way, covering work such as making steps and boardwalks, and trimming back trees.
Appointing key staff	Key staff can be appointed to 'advise and assist' the public on open land where the owner and occupier are agreeable. Staff can also be appointed to ensure that the public comply with bylaws or the Litter Act 1958. They can also be employed to ensure paths are well defined and maintained or carry out such duties as the local authority determine.

Provision of advice on nature conservation	Duty of all local authorities to bring to the attention of the public, and of schoolchildren in particular, the provisions of the Wildlife and Countryside Act towards the protection of birds, animals and plants.
Nature conservation duties	Local authorities are required to 'have regard to the desirability of conserving the natural beauty and amenity of the countryside' and urged to take nature conservation into account when managing land.

(Source: London Ecology Unit, 1990)

Within councils, there may be many employees whose work impinges on the management of urban habitats, as indicated in Table 2.3 (overleaf). They can be divided broadly into three groups: those concerned mainly with planning, such as recreation planners; those concerned mainly with project design, such as landscape architects and civil engineers; and those concerned with land management and maintenance, such as parks managers. The way in which these responsibilities and positions are split between departments varies considerably between local authorities, as does the extent of internal liaison over environmental matters. The more enlightened local authorities have a publicly stated corporate policy on landscape and nature conservation, and in some cases actively promote internal liaison on environmental matters by the formation of environmental committees or project groups that cross departmental boundaries.

Table 2.3 Local authority employees whose work may concern urban habitats

Strategic planning	Planners	Town planners
		Economic planners
		Mineral planners
		Environmental planners
		Recreation planners
		Urban designers
		Landscape planners
		Development control
Design and development	Ecologists	
	Architects	
	Landscape architects	
	Surveyors	
	Engineers	Civil
		Municipal
		Highway
		Clerk of works
		Landscape clerk of works
Management	Environmental Health Officers	
	Open space managers	Estate managers
		Parks managers
		Recreation managers
		Horticulturists
		Maintenance staff
		Foresters
		Rangers/wardens
		Conservation staff
	Public relations officers	
	Teachers	

(Source: Simmons, Pocock and Barker, 1990)

If you would like to raise a matter about urban land use but are uncertain who to contact, senior officers concerned with planning and land use, or recreation and leisure, are most likely to be able to help in the first instance. The local education authority may be able to help if the enquiry involves the use of sites by schools.

2.5 Liaison and partnership

In the same way that individuals can gain by working in groups, and departments within a local authority can gain by internal collaboration, so groups and organisations can gain by working together. This applies to links not only between different voluntary groups, but also, for example, between groups, local authorities, businesses and private and public sector landowners.

At the simplest level, liaison involves sharing and exchanging information. Your group may have to be very active at first in initiating a link, in both seeking and supplying information, but once trust is established simple mechanisms can usually be set up by which relevant information is automatically shared.

Liaison is facilitated if some members of the group also belong to other groups or work for the local authority, but there are many other ways of building up links. There may be informal 'green networks', whereby local groups exchange news, newsletters, programmes of events and minutes of meetings. Your group can invite members of other groups, or local authority officers or councillors, to give a talk, or organise occasional joint meetings. You can establish more formal links by affiliation or by establishing joint committees on which members from several groups and organisations are represented.

Liaison with similar groups in other areas can be achieved by affiliation with a national organisation, which itself is likely to have strong contacts with other related organisations.

Many local authorities are keen to build strong links with community groups, but your group may have to take the initiative. You should familiarise yourself with the structure of the local authority, the relevant committees, and key personnel and councillors concerned with issues relating to nature conservation. Much of this information can be found in council year-books, which are usually held by public libraries. You should also familiarise yourself with council policies concerning urban nature conservation by consulting published policy documents such as **structure**, **local** and **green plans**.

Local authority

Your group can ask to be placed on the local authority's mailing list of those consulted on planning policies and development applications. You can bring particular sites to the attention of the local authority by providing detailed information about the wildlife value of sites in your area and about the way in which they are used and valued by the community. You can volunteer to undertake specific tasks on behalf of the authority, such as planting trees, or offer to manage a local site. Under the system of **compulsory competitive tendering (CCT),** in which all authorities whose expenditure on ground maintenance exceeds a certain threshold are required to put their work out to tender, your group can bid for a contract to undertake regular site maintenance, or lobby for a more ecological approach to be specified in the maintenance contract for a particular site.

In many areas there are well-established mechanisms for liaison between the local authority and local groups on matters concerning urban nature conservation. For example, in the London Borough of Camden, representatives from voluntary groups are invited to attend the meetings of the council's environmental working parties as advisers. Reading Borough Council has appointed a liaison officer to co-ordinate the work of volunteers in the community, which also serves to sustain interest and momentum within the council. In Leicester there is an Ecology Advisory Group that has representatives from the City Council, the County Council, the Leicester and Rutland Trust for Nature Conservation and the City Wildlife Project. This group was set up to prepare an **ecology strategy** and oversee its implementation. The local authority officers on the joint group report back directly to council committees, so ensuring that the group's views carry weight. In Leeds, a nature conservation forum was set up to seek the advice and comments of local voluntary groups on the city council's **nature conservation strategy**. Joint nature conservation committees and forums are most likely to be worthwhile and productive if, as in these examples, they have a clear brief.

Often joint steering committees, involving representatives from local authorities, local residents and voluntary groups for example, are established to oversee the management of particular sites. Examples of the role and composition of such committees for two wildlife sites in London are shown in Table 2.4 (overleaf).

Table 2.4 Role and composition of the management committees for two wildlife sites in London

	Hither Green Nature Reserve	Camley Street Natural Park
Main functions	• To prepare and administer management plan • To keep records of conservation and survey work • To be responsible for accommodation and equipment • To control access to the reserve	• To oversee implementation of management plan • To ensure that legal responsibilities are followed • To be responsible for warden • To allow involvement of various interest groups • To consider financial matters, conservation management, access, education, building maintenance, interpretation and publicity
Meetings per year	Six	Six
Composition	Members: • representative from community and residents' group • representative from local schools • representative from local naturalists • representative from education authority • representative from London Wildlife Trust, Lewisham group • local residents Ex-officio: • local ward councillors • officers of Planning and Parks Departments of London Borough of Lewisham • warden of London Borough of Lewisham Nature Centre	Members: • vice-chair of London Wildlife Trust (LWT) • representative from LWT Development Committee • representative from LWT Education Committee • LWT Deputy Director (Conservation) • representative from Camley Street Support Group (local volunteers) Co-opted members: • two Camden councillors • representative from education • two representatives from Support Group Advisers: • officer from London Ecology Unit • officer from London Borough of Camden Works Department • officer from London Borough of Camden Planning Department • interpretative consultant
Responsible to	London Borough of Lewisham Leisure Services Committee and Planning and Transport Committee	LWT Conservation Committee

(Source: London Ecology Unit, 1990)

Police

In urban areas particularly, it is helpful to liaise with the police. All areas have police wildlife liaison officers and in some areas, such as Dudley, there are 'Wildlife Watch' schemes whereby local people help police keep an eye on sites. That apart, the police are essential to help deal with any anti-social incidents, and community police are often happy to join in with local people to help set up and manage projects.

Groundwork Trusts

The network of Groundwork Trusts and their umbrella organisation, the Groundwork Foundation, have been established specifically to promote the partnership of all sectors of the community in improving the urban environment. The first Groundwork projects, initiated by the Countryside

Commission and funded by the Department of the Environment, local authorities and the Commission, concentrated on improving opportunities for public recreation in the urban fringe, but projects now include the restoration of derelict land within towns and cities. The projects are run by locally based independent trusts with management boards drawn from local authorities, landowners, industrialists and the local community. Each trust has a core of professional staff, including landscape architects, whose role is to involve, co-ordinate, advise and generally support local people in schemes to improve the local environment. Initially, the distribution of Groundwork Trusts was biased towards the north of England where the scheme was piloted, but one of the main roles of the Groundwork Foundation is to help set up new trusts country-wide.

In some large conurbations, wildlife units set up by former metropolitan councils have survived as liaison and advisory units, now jointly funded by several borough councils. Examples include the Greater Manchester Countryside Unit and the London Ecology Unit.

Wildlife unit

2.6 Adopting an area-wide nature conservation strategy

Because of the high value of urban land, wildlife sites in towns and cities are often the subject of repeated applications for planning permission to develop them for other uses. In some cases, local authorities have found themselves powerless to prevent undesirable developments on urban open space because the planning guidelines given in their policy documents have not been specific enough. In others, the value of a piece of open ground to local people, and to wildlife, has not been fully appreciated until the site has been threatened with development. By that time, a local campaign may be too late to influence decisions about the site's use.

It is very much better to be in a position to anticipate developments rather than simply respond to events after they have happened. For this reason, many local authorities have now completed at least a preliminary survey of their nature conservation resource, and have used this as a basis for drawing up an area-wide nature conservation strategy incorporating planning guidelines for broad categories of wildlife sites.

In some cases, local authorities have employed professional ecologists to carry out their wildlife habitat survey, but in many places local wildlife trusts and groups have initiated the surveys and played a large part in carrying them out, as in Reading and Sheffield. Some surveys have depended largely on the help of volunteers from the general public working under professional guidance, as in Brighton. Usually the surveys have been undertaken as a team effort, with the local authority or wildlife trust taking the lead but calling on a variety of sources of local expertise.

If your local authority has yet to carry out an area-wide survey, you could suggest that they undertake one and offer to help. In places where preliminary surveys have already been done, there may be a need to extend the survey area, to provide more detailed information on particular species or sites, or to update existing records. Initially the local authority may be wary of such an approach from local groups, especially if they have experience of developments that have been halted mid-stream by local campaigns. But if your group can build up a detailed knowledge of a local wildlife site or sites before any development is proposed, it is likely to be viewed as a valuable source of information and treated with some respect.

2.7 Exercise 2: Establishing how you can work together

1   Make a list of the local groups which might have an interest in urban nature conservation and the management of open space in your area, by consulting the local library or planning department. Determine the aims, objectives and activities of the groups by reading their publicity material or contacting group officials, and single out any groups that have aims related to your own.

2   Make brief notes on the policies of the local authority concerning urban open space and nature conservation by consulting their published statements such as local plans and environmental strategy documents.

3   Find out about, and keep a record of, the local authority officers and councillors most closely involved with nature conservation and environmental education issues.

2.8 Case study examples of two local groups

The Pensnett Wildlife Group

The Pensnett Wildlife Group was started by the arrival of a great northern diver at Fens Pools one Christmas. This bird, which stayed for several weeks, attracted several hundred bird-watchers to the site, an area containing feeder pools for the Stourbridge Canal system in the heart of the Black Country.

Once mainly farmland, the site has been mined for coal and used for tipping slag from the nearby steel works. The area that is unsuitable for building or industrial use has gradually been reclaimed by nature. Its mosaic of pools, reed-swamp, ponds, marsh, grassland and scrub is unique in the Dudley district and provides a 'green lung' in the heart of an intensively developed area.

The stir caused by the presence of the rare bird brought home to people the potential of the site and its interest for local bird-watchers. With rumours rife that the pools were about to be sold, drained, filled in or otherwise developed, one local bird-watcher decided to call a meeting of all those interested in preserving the area. Since bird-watchers have an effective web of communication for passing on or receiving information on rare bird sightings, publicising the meeting was easy.

At the first official meeting, 19 people were present and the Pensnett Wildlife Group was formed. For the first few meetings the group had the help of a member of the Urban Wildlife Group who had done a basic survey of the habitats and helped set out some proposals for the future. At the second meeting there were 27 people and the usual officers and committee were elected. At the third meeting, attendance increased to 40 people and the group was up and away.

The annual subscription started at £1 (50p if unemployed and many were) and a meeting charge of 30p. The meeting place was and still is the Pensnett Conservative Club – not a hint of politics but a pleasant and informal atmosphere, which is the key to successful meetings. The group is not charged for the use of the room but does make concerted efforts to boost the bar takings.

The group's long-term aim has been to have the Fens Pools designated as a Local Nature Reserve with a fully operational wardening service. After six years it is part way towards achieving this aim. The area is now well wardened, at least during weekdays. The site, initially designated by the local authority as a Grade B **Site of Importance for Nature Conservation (SINC)**, was later upgraded to Grade A. It has now been designated a **Site of Special Scientific Interest (SSSI)**, thanks mainly to survey work by one of the members on amphibians, which showed the site had a good population of the rare great crested newt. It is acknowledged as the best amphibian site in the West Midlands, but until a problem of ownership of part of the area has been resolved the council cannot declare the site a Local Nature Reserve.

A strong membership helps with conservation work and raises money for conservation projects. The committee realised early on that this required a 'carrot-and-stick approach'. It provides carrots in the form of varied wildlife talks every month, usually illustrated by slides, and field trips by car, minibus or coach to nature reserves across Great Britain. At least nine members have given talks, quite often for the first time in their lives. In return the committee tries to get as many members as possible involved in practical conservation work such as litter round-ups, running a tree nursery, survey work on birds, amphibians, flowers, fungi, etc., and construction of floating islands for roosting and nesting water-birds.

The first island was designed and produced as an examination project by a local school. It was made to look natural with turfs and willow, which grew well until a high wind turned over the raft. This did not deter a coot and a great crested grebe from nesting and raising families on the upturned raft.

Another project involved creating a wild butterfly garden in a sheltered valley by planting nectar-producing shrubs and providing seeds of larval food plants for group members to raise for transplanting into the butterfly garden. The group has also had an additional pond dug for amphibians, and fenced other ponds to keep out horses with the help of a grant from the local authority.

One of the group's biggest efforts has been in getting the local children involved. Numerous nature walks have been undertaken to show children the plants, trees and birds. The group even staged a wildlife exhibition in a large marquee provided by the local council, which over 700 children from local primary schools attended – a chaotic and rewarding day!

The group has produced a booklet designed to encourage children from the six local primary schools to visit the reserve. Called 'Look Out & About', it comprises pictures, descriptions and questions on a range of plants and animals that they should find in the reserve, in an 'I-Spy' format. The display department of the local council has helped with the design of the cover and a lapel badge and the Nature Conservation Consultative Group has given a grant towards the printing costs.

The group describes itself as a 'soft pressure group'. Working with the officers of the local authority has produced results. It is perhaps lucky in that Dudley Metropolitan Borough Council has always been interested in conservation. The group is represented on the Nature Conservation Consultative Group, a liaison group comprising local councillors, council officials and wildlife groups. It is also represented on the Fens/Buckpool Steering Committee which oversees the management of the reserve. It tries to keep the local council aware of its activities and aspirations through personal contacts, committees and a quarterly newsletter.

In general, the group tries to keep its aims and efforts well publicised. The local press is always hungry for news and the group provides what it can: '£500 Reward for Swan Killer', etc. It has a mobile display, which depicts the glories of the Fens Pools and the group's basic aims. The group has even appeared on television.

Their advice to others thinking about joining or forming a local group is just go ahead. 'Setting up and running a successful wildlife group depends on a sense of purpose and enthusiasm rather than skill and efficiency. If you have an area you think worth trying to preserve, badger your local council, contact the press and get the support of anyone you can. Don't be downhearted by setbacks. Even if you fail in your objective at least you will have the advantage of knowing that you tried. At Fens Pools, it's a wonderful feeling on a warm summer evening watching the family of great crested grebes, knowing we did our bit to protect the pool they call home.'

(Source: Gareth Barton and Brian Jones, Pensnett Wildlife Group)

Friends of Forest Lane Park

The Friends of Forest Lane Park are helping to establish a wildlife area in the grounds of the old Forest Gate Maternity Hospital, now being redeveloped, in the London Borough of Newham.

When the redundant hospital was closed in 1985, rapidly escalating land prices prevented Newham Council from buying the site to be used as a park as they had originally intended. Instead, they could only stipulate that developers should retain a proportion of the site as open space, and pay for the development of a park, in return for outline planning permission for houses on three-fifths of the site.

After public consultation, proposals for a fairly formal park layout for the site were adopted. But one local resident, a former teacher with experience of environmental projects, felt that there was scope for a more imaginative scheme with greater community involvement. As a result of discussing her ideas with friends and acquaintances, an informal group began to meet in each others' homes to share their ideas for the site.

Calling themselves at that time the 'Friends for Nature', their proposals were to retain part of the site as a wild area, which could be used for wildlife study by local schools. They organised a public meeting in a local school with residents and parents to discuss ideas to put forward to the park's planners. They obtained enthusiastic letters of support for their proposals from local junior and infant schools, a nursery school and Newham Pre-School Playgroup Association. They invited the Trust for Urban Ecology to carry out a preliminary survey of the site, assess its potential for educational purposes and suggest how the site could be managed.

Armed with these letters of support and information about the site's potential, they successfully put their case to the Leisure Services Committee of Newham Council, who agreed to retain the more wooded southern edge of the site as a wildlife area and educational facility.

In the following months the group held a series of open meetings in a local school, with speakers invited from the Parks Department and the Highways Department, and talks by the Tree Officer, the Project Officer and the Chair of Planning from Newham Council. They also invited the site manager for the local health authority and the Director of the Trust for Urban Ecology to give talks.

A plan for the wildlife area was drawn up by the council's landscape architect. It included a woodland area that preserved existing trees, a wildflower meadow, and a shallow pond. There was also to be an under-sevens' playground. The plan for the more formal part of the park included formal gardens, a small lake, and grassed areas for games and leisure (see Figure 2.1).

There then followed a two-year lull while details of the sale of the site were settled. When the developers finally moved onto the site, the group once more became active. After further meetings to discuss site proposals with the landscape architect, the Newham Community Trees Project and representatives from local schools, the group was relaunched with an open day and work party session on the site to publicise the plans to the local community and encourage their participation and support.

The reconstituted group have adopted a new name, 'Friends of Forest Lane Park'. They have become affiliated to the British Trust for Conservation Volunteers and have agreed a written constitution. Their committee has a chair, a secretary and a treasurer, with the power to co-opt up to six more members. They have set out their aims and objectives as follows.

'The aim of the group is to improve and enhance the nature area of the new park for the benefit of wildlife and local people, including schools and voluntary groups. To fulfil this aim the group will be affiliated to the British Trust for Conservation Volunteers (BTCV) and will undertake the following activities:

▶ promoting and carrying out practical conservation work on the site;

▶ educating volunteers in the principles and practices of conservation;

▶ providing information on the area.'

They have since organised a series of work sessions on the site, providing refreshments for the volunteers and encouraging visitors to come and see what is going on. Activities have included clearing up litter, pruning a laurel hedge, clearing invasive brambles and sycamore saplings, constructing two large compost bins from salvaged fencing, setting up a tree nursery, rescuing bulbs from the part of the site to be redeveloped, and fencing off vulnerable areas to protect them from damage by the contracters. Children and parent members of the local Woodcraft Folk group have helped construct bird and bat boxes to attach to the mature trees.

Affiliation with BTCV has brought benefits of cheap insurance, small start-up grants and access to tools, information and advice through the Newham Community Trees Project that BTCV administers on behalf of the council. Newham Council has recently approved a grant to the group to purchase their own tools, although the problem of secure storage of tools on the site has yet to be resolved.

Now that the wildlife area is beginning to take shape, members have visited local schools with displays and information and are encouraging school groups to visit the site. One local school is helping to produce badges to publicise the site. The Parks Department and Leisure Services have invited the group to a meeting to discuss plans for an ecology study centre in the old gatehouse lodge. Although the core of committed members find it hard work to maintain the momentum and the active involvement of others, they at least have the satisfaction of knowing that they are well on the way to achieving their original aims.

(Source: Mary Young and Maureen Wood, Friends of Forest Lane Park)

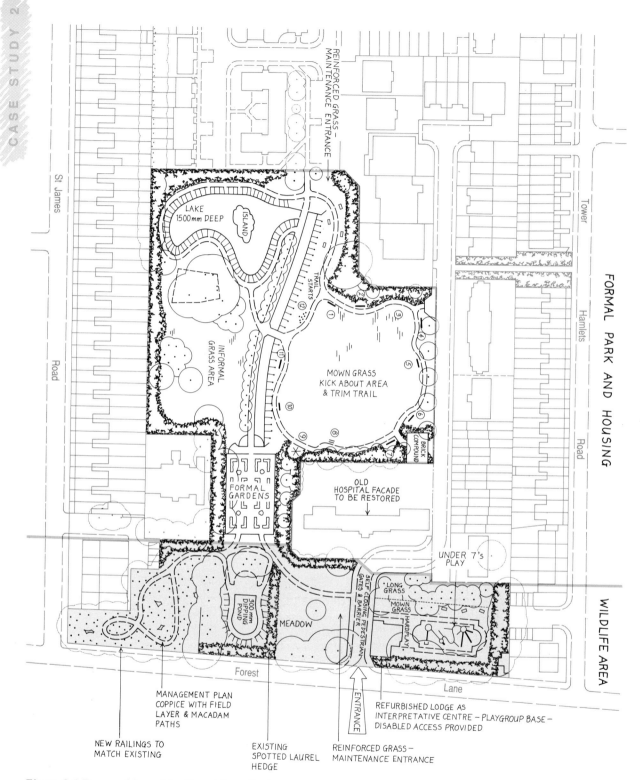

Figure 2.1 Proposed layout for Forest Lane Park

The following labels appear within the figure:

- REINFORCED GRASS – MAINTENANCE ENTRANCE
- LAKE 1500mm DEEP
- ISLAND
- TRAIL STARTS
- INFORMAL GRASS AREA
- MOWN GRASS KICK ABOUT AREA & TRIM TRAIL
- BRICK COMPOUND
- FORMAL GARDENS
- OLD HOSPITAL FACADE TO BE RESTORED
- UNDER 7's PLAY
- LONG GRASS
- MOWN GRASS
- SELF CLOSING PEDESTRIAN GATES & BARRIER
- HARDPLAY
- 300mm DIPPING POND
- MEADOW
- St James Road
- Tower Hamlets Road
- FORMAL PARK AND HOUSING
- WILDLIFE AREA
- Forest Lane
- ENTRANCE
- MANAGEMENT PLAN COPPICE WITH FIELD LAYER & MACADAM PATHS
- NEW RAILINGS TO MATCH EXISTING
- EXISTING SPOTTED LAUREL HEDGE
- REINFORCED GRASS – MAINTENANCE ENTRANCE
- REFURBISHED LODGE AS INTERPRETATIVE CENTRE – PLAYGROUP BASE – DISABLED ACCESS PROVIDED

Chapter 3

ASSESSING SITES FOR THEIR VALUE FOR WILDLIFE

An assessment of the existing value of sites, both for wildlife and to the community, is an essential first step in any decisions about how sites should be managed. This applies equally to decisions made by a local authority about sites throughout an area and to those taken by community groups concerned mainly about the management of a particular site.

If you belong to a large group or one which has members with specialist knowledge, and a comprehensive wildlife habitat survey has yet to be done in your town or city, you may decide to initiate an area-wide survey. However, this is a considerable undertaking and requires close liaison with the local authority and the support of as many other local organisations or individuals as possible. If your group is relatively small, and more concerned with sites in the immediate neighbourhood, you may decide to limit your activities to a more detailed local survey, calling on help and expert advice from larger groups and the local authority as necessary.

If your group is interested mainly in the management of one particular site, then a site-specific survey will be most relevant, although other local sites might be checked to ensure there is not a more appropriate site for the group's purposes nearby. The local authority or an experienced group such as a local wildlife trust may be able to advise you if your group would like to become involved with the management of a wildlife site but does not have a particular site in mind.

The systematic assessment of sites throughout an area for their value as wildlife habitat is usually described as a two-phase process, although in practice in urban areas the phases often overlap:

▶ **Phase I** (area-wide) involves a preliminary survey, partly desk-based, to identify the main areas of open space throughout an area, and to map their dominant vegetation.

▶ **Phase II** (site-specific) involves a more detailed assessment of individual sites, listing the plant (and sometimes animal) species present.

The first phase provides basic information on the nature, distribution and extent of wildlife areas. This information can be used to formulate local authority planning documents that provide guidelines for planning application decisions, as mentioned in Chapter 2. It can also indicate sites that merit more detailed survey. The second phase, as well as providing additional valuable input to any planning decisions concerning specific sites, provides a sound basis for decisions about the most appropriate form of management and for the development of visitor information and educational material about a site. In all cases, the information from the wildlife surveys needs to be supplemented by information about the social value of sites, as described in Chapter 4.

In practice, the scale of wildlife habitat surveys, the number of phases and their level of detail are usually determined by the resources available (in terms of people, expertise, funds and time) and by the purpose of those responsible for the survey. Whatever the scale of the survey you undertake, it is good practice to adopt standard procedures so that the information you collect will be compatible with other surveys and can be readily communicated to other people.

This chapter describes the main factors that influence the type of vegetation and animals found on urban sites, to help you recognise the signs that suggest that one site may be more valuable for wildlife than another, and explains how to carry out a wildlife habitat survey. It includes a practical exercise in habitat assessment for you to do, and illustrates the process of habitat assessment with a case study example.

3.1 Factors that influence a site's value for wildlife

Urban habitats differ from rural ones in both the scale and the intensity of human impacts on them. These affect wildlife by their influence on physical conditions, such as soils and climate, and on ecological processes, such as colonisation, succession, nutrition and reproduction. Site conditions may be subject to rapid rates of change because of the pressures of development and changes in ownership and management.

Physical conditions

Soil structure

The soils of many urban sites are characterised by disturbance and variability. This is particularly true of old industrial land and demolition sites. Even sites that have escaped development, such as remnants of woodland and old grassland, may have been disturbed in places by tipping and excavation. Most land will have been significantly modified by development.

In old gardens, parks and allotments, the topsoil may be deep, well structured and fertile as a result of a build-up of organic matter, but in many urban sites subsoil and even parent rock may be exposed as a result of development. The soil may be further modified by the addition of material such as industrial and domestic waste, brick rubble, and topsoil imported from other areas. All these modifications influence the type of vegetation cover that can develop.

pH

In particular, soil disturbance can alter the **pH** of a site, which is a measure of the acidity or alkalinity of the soil. Many industrial wastes, and the mortar, cement and plaster in brick rubble, are alkaline, so that urban sites where these materials have been incorporated tend to be alkaline, as shown in Table 3.1 for sites in Greater Manchester. Alkaline conditions encourage the development of lime-loving plants, or **calcicoles**, such as old man's beard and centaury. Since calcareous habitats such as chalk and limestone grasslands do not occur naturally in the Manchester area, the Leblanc waste sites there are considered particularly interesting and important habitats.

A few waste materials, such as furnace ash and cinders, and acid subsoils when exposed or disturbed so that they occur at the surface, create more acid conditions, allowing the establishment of heathland plants such as heather (ling), broom and sheep's sorrel.

Sometimes the variation in pH across a site caused by disturbance leads to unusual associations of plants that would not normally be found in the wild. For example, at Stoney Hill in Telford, common spotted orchids have colonised the alkaline clay subsoil left from opencast mining, alongside clubmosses, more characteristic of mountainous areas, that are growing on very acid spoil.

Table 3.1 Types of industrial waste forming calcareous plant habitats in Greater Manchester

Material and origin	Initial pH
Leblanc process alkali waste from manufacture of sodium carbonate	Up to 12.7
Blast furnace slag from smelting of iron ores	Up to 10.6
Pulverised fuel ash from coal-burning power stations	Up to 9.5
Calcium carbonate slurry from chemical works	Up to 8.6
Calcareous boiler ash	Up to 8.2
Colliery washery waste	Up to 8.0
Calcareous colliery spoil	Up to 8.0
Demolition rubble	Up to 7.8

(Source: Gemmell, 1982)

Nutrients

The main nutrients needed for plant growth are nitrogen (in the form of nitrate), phosphorus and potassium. Phosphorus and potassium are present in the clay used to make bricks, so are usually adequately supplied by brick rubble on old building sites, but nitrate-nitrogen is likely to be deficient until some organic matter begins to accumulate and decay. This deficiency slows down the growth of most plants on demolition sites but favours **legumes**, such as clovers and vetches, since they have root nodules containing bacteria that can 'fix' nitrate from gaseous nitrogen in the soil.

The pH of a site can affect the availability of the nutrients that are present. Within the pH range 6.5–8 most nutrients remain available, so soils that are fertile and neutral or moderately alkaline promote plant growth but may allow a few more vigorous species to dominate all others. Sites where the nutrient supply is limited may therefore support a more diverse or unusual community of plant species.

Compaction

Many urban sites suffer from soil compaction, as a result of frequent traffic from vehicles and people. This can impede soil aeration and drainage, reducing plant vigour, and favouring the growth of tolerant plants such as creeping buttercup and creeping bent. Where compaction results in waterlogging, it can encourage wetland species, such as rushes and marsh foxtail.

Climate

There can be a marked difference in climate between built-up areas and the surrounding countryside, as summarised in Figure 3.1 (overleaf). The centres of large towns and cities are generally slightly warmer than the surrounding countryside, as a result of heat stored by buildings and roads and trapped in the dusty atmosphere. The cooling effect associated with vegetation is lost as green areas are built over. The warmer urban conditions can encourage early flowering, extend the growing season and reduce the risk of frost. The extra warmth may also encourage birds to nest early and make urban sites attractive as roosts and overwintering sites.

Occasionally the heat generated by an industry can allow the survival of species normally restricted to warmer climates, as in the case of the fig trees growing along the River Don in Sheffield, described in Box 3.1 (overleaf).

Urban areas tend to be more overcast and receive more rainfall than the surrounding countryside, especially in areas downwind of heavy industry,

Urban		Rural
+ 0.5–3°C		Mean temperature
- 5–15%		Sunshine
+ 5–10%		Cloud
+ 10–20%		Storms
- 6%		Mean humidity

Figure 3.1   Summary of some of the differences in climatic conditions between urban and rural areas

Box 3.1   Wild figs by the River Don

For a long time the wild figs that grew by the River Don in Sheffield went unnoticed. It took some time for local botanists to realise that to find fig trees in such numbers is very unusual in Great Britain. A detailed vegetation survey along the river bank revealed 35 trees. All are well-grown specimens with numerous stems so that they appear like globular shrubs up to 8 metres high and rather more across. This is quite different from their growth form in the Mediterranean where they have a single stout trunk.

Although they produce crops of green figs, the fruits do not open and in any case could not be pollinated as the fig wasp pollinator does not occur in Great Britain. Most types of cultivated fig can ripen their fruits in the absence of pollination, but the fruits of the River Don figs abort before they are ripe.

The figs have proved difficult to age precisely; since there is sometimes more than one flush of growth in a year the growth rings counted in cores bored from the trunk do not correspond to annual rings. It is estimated that many are at least 60–70 years old. No young trees have been seen.

The origin of the figs is known – seeds derived from sewage. During rainy periods, combined storm and foul water sewers become overloaded and raw sewage enters the river as it has done for hundreds of years. But sewage enters most of our large rivers and the consumption of figs is not restricted to Sheffield.

The trees are more numerous at the east end of the city, and this points to a connection with heavy industry. Since no young fig trees occur, it appears

that conditions are no longer suitable for their establishment. This and the Mediterranean distribution of the species suggest that the period when the figs established coincided with the height of the steel industry. At that time river water was used for cooling and the Don ran at a constant 20°C. In the last few years, following the collapse of the steel industry, river temperatures have been much lower, but mature trees are able to survive.

This historical explanation, if correct, means that the wild figs of Sheffield are as much a part of its industrial heritage as Bessemer converters, steam hammers and crucible steel.

(Source: Gilbert and Pearman, 1988)

as updrafts of warm air cool and condense out on particulate matter in the atmosphere. Often the rain occurs as storms in which most of the water is lost as run-off from hard surfaces and little percolates into the soil. Heavy demand for water for industrial and domestic purposes means that the normal groundwater level is likely to be low. Conditions on urban sites therefore tend to be dry. The rapid discharge of large amounts of storm water into drains can overload urban sewage works, causing the pollution of watercourses and damaging aquatic wildlife. Storm water management by the incorporation of small retention ponds and marshes into new developments, and by the avoidance of impermeable surfaces wherever possible, can reduce run-off, increase groundwater recharge and provide additional wildlife habitat.

Air pollution

The main air-borne pollutants affecting wildlife in urban areas are, or at least have been until recently, sulphur dioxide and smoke. Even though smokeless zones have been established in city centres and a decline in traditional industries has checked pollution in some areas, the levels present may still be sufficient to affect some animals and plants. Previously high levels may have long-lasting effects, for example by limiting the number and type of mature trees now present in industrial cities.

Sulphur dioxide, produced when coal or oil is burned, damages leaf tissue and increases the acidity of soil. Many coniferous trees are particularly sensitive to sulphur dioxide, especially species of pine, spruce and fir. Beech and oak are also fairly sensitive. A few tree species are pollution-tolerant, for example Manchester poplar, hybrid black poplar, crack and white willows, plane, and to some extent ash and sycamore.

Lichens show a wide range of sensitivity to sulphur dioxide pollution, and the distribution of different species can be used as an indicator of pollution levels. Many are extremely sensitive to sulphur dioxide but one, *Lecanora conizaeoides*, is unusually tolerant and so has been able to spread in urban areas as more sensitive types have declined. The impact of sulphur dioxide pollution on the lichen cover of tree trunks has contributed to the occurrence of unusually dark forms of some moths in urban areas, as described in Box 3.2 (overleaf).

Smoke affects plants mainly because it reduces light intensity and so restricts photosynthesis. Particulate matter in the smoke can coat leaves and clog the leaf pores. The result may be stunted growth, early leaf fall in deciduous trees, leaf fall in trees that are normally evergreen (such as privet and holly), and reduced accumulation of food reserves in bulbs so that they fail to flower.

In recent years, nitrous oxides and hydrocarbons from vehicle exhausts have become an increasingly important cause of pollution, contributing to ozone formation and affecting people's health. As yet, the impact on vegetation is unclear, but it probably places additional stresses on sensitive plants, especially in the presence of other pollutants. In particular, some tree species may be debilitated.

Soil contamination

Urban soils (and air) may be contaminated with high levels of heavy metals such as copper, lead, zinc and boron from sources such as ash, refuse, sewage sludge, vehicle exhausts and industrial processes. This can severely restrict the activity of micro-organisms in the soil, slowing down the decay of organic matter and the recycling of nutrients on urban sites.

There may be localised effects on vegetation as a result of the use of salt to keep roads free of ice in winter. Heavy application of salt has allowed some maritime

Box 3.2 Melanism in urban moths

One of the more publicised aspects of urban ecology is the indirect effect of air pollution in promoting **melanism** (darker forms) among moths. As tree trunks lose their lichen cover (from sulphur dioxide pollution) and become blackened (with soot), species such as the light coloured peppered moth, which normally spend the day resting on the bark relying on cryptic colouration to avoid detection, suddenly become conspicuous to predators. Under this selection pressure the rare black form begins to increase in number relative to the usual pale form as it is now well camouflaged on the dark tree trunks. Since melanism is inherited, by the 1950s the great majority of peppered moths in urban areas were black, though in country areas the pale form remained commonest. The same effect is quite widespread among nocturnal moths that rest on tree trunks during the day, such as the pale brindled beauty, scalloped hazel, waved umber, grey dagger and mottled beauty.

Over the period from 1973 to 1986 there has been a revival in the proportion of the paler form of the peppered moth in the outer areas of industrial cities such as Manchester, although the grey lichens that formed the cryptic background have so far not returned. However, there has been an increase in the abundance of the pollution-tolerant lichen *Lecanora*

conizaeoides, which does not form a protective background for either form, so it could be that both forms of peppered moth are now equally at a disadvantage.
(Source: Gilbert, 1989)

species, such as reflexed salt-marsh-grass, to grow along the roadside verges of some inland towns. Urban trees may occasionally be killed if they are close to a point where road salt is stored. The leaves of roadside vegetation may be scorched by salt spray and salt-sensitive plants may die out.

Water pollution

Water pollution is common in urban areas and can have profound effects on aquatic wildlife. The discharge of excessive amounts of untreated or partially treated sewage into rivers, and its breakdown by micro-organisms, can create anaerobic conditions in which only the most tolerant species can survive. Sewage also enriches the level of nutrients in the water, a process termed **eutrophication**, which stimulates the growth of algae and further depletes the water of oxygen as the algae decay. A similar process of eutrophication can occur in urban lakes or reservoirs where large numbers of waterfowl or gulls congregate; examples can be found in park lakes in central London and St Albans where the accumulated faeces of waterfowl form a deep layer of sediment.

Storm water run-off can increase the turbidity of watercourses, by increasing the levels of suspended matter, so reducing light levels for submerged aquatic plants and affecting the respiration of invertebrates and fish. The dust and debris washed into the water during storms means that small bodies of still water, such as ponds, rapidly silt up.

Chemicals discharged into watercourses by industry, such as heavy metals and organic compounds, can seriously affect all forms of aquatic wildlife.

Pesticide use tends to be localised in urban areas. Although herbicides may be routinely used to control weeds in formal planting schemes, and along paths, roadsides and railway tracks, many other areas remain pesticide-free. Some attractive and formerly common arable weeds that have now been almost eliminated from farmland by frequent and widespread herbicide use may survive in urban allotments and gardens. Where no insecticides are used and other conditions are suitable, urban gardens may support very large numbers of insect species; for example, over 300 different species of moths and butterflies have been recorded in one garden in Leicester and over 700 species of beetle in a long-term study of a garden in Blackheath in London.

Ecological factors

Colonisation of bare ground by plants relies mainly on the **seed bank** (the seeds already present on the site in the soil) and the **seed rain** (seeds which arrive at the site from elsewhere, for example blown in by the wind). Areas of vegetation established before urban development occurred will have had plentiful nearby sources of seed for colonisation, but the variety of plant species colonising recently disturbed urban sites may be limited by isolation from seed sources. The most commonly occurring species on disturbed urban sites are those which produce large numbers of wind-dispersed seeds, such as rosebay willowherb, coltsfoot, ragwort and goat willow.

These plants may be augmented by those which are transported to the site by people. Seeds of wild plants may be brought in with the soil carried on footwear and vehicle tyres, or in topsoil used to grade out, or level, a site. If a site is landscaped, seeds may be introduced with the soil on the roots of nursery-grown shrubs and trees, or with bark and peat mulch. Wildflower seed mixtures may be deliberately sown.

Human-mediated dispersal also accounts for the presence of species that are not normally found growing in the wild in this country. These **introduced species**, many of which are garden plants, are a characteristic feature of many disturbed urban sites. Some are spread by the dumping of garden waste; examples include golden rod, Michaelmas daisy, Japanese knotweed and spotted dead-nettle. Some garden plants may persist where housing has been demolished; common examples include garden mints, Virginia creeper, Boston ivy and Russian vine. A few species, such as millet, may arrive in the seed mixtures used to feed birds.

In industrial areas, raw materials and waste provide a further source of introduced plants. For example, seeds from Australasia, Africa, South America and the Mediterranean have been introduced with imported fleeces used by the wool industry. The pirri-pirri bur, originally from Australia, has been introduced to some areas in this way. Seeds of North African plants have arrived in the waste cotton rags used by the paper industry. Some seeds have been introduced with the oilseeds used in the oil-milling industry, many of which are supplied from North America. Examples include sunflower, *Amaranthus paniculatus*, *Artemesia biennis* and fox-tail barley. Seeds of plants such as the warty-cabbage and bastard cabbage have been introduced with grain imported by flour mills and breweries. Imported species are particularly likely to be found in old railway goods yards and dockside areas; London Docks support several tropical and sub-tropical legumes. Most introduced species rely on repeated introduction for their persistence. A few, such as Oxford ragwort, Japanese knotweed and pirri-pirri bur, have become thoroughly established and spread.

The plant species that colonise the bare ground of disturbed sites are termed **ruderals**. They tend to be plants that flourish under conditions of intermittent disturbance, little grazing pressure or competition, and alkaline soils. Most are **annual** or **biennial**. Annuals complete their life cycle in one year, germinating from seed, flowering, setting seed and dying in the same growing season. Biennials take two years to complete this cycle, flowering and setting seed in the second year. Because they are short-lived species, annuals and biennials rely on the production of large numbers of seeds for their survival.

Once some form of vegetation becomes established on a disturbed site, the soil structure develops and fertility increases. After 3 to 6 years, tall **perennial** grasses and herbs, which die down to the ground in the autumn but produce new shoots each year, gradually spread and compete with the annuals and biennials. The proportion of grasses increases with time, so that after 8 or 10 years a grassland with scattered tall herbs develops. If the site remains undisturbed, shrubs and trees may eventually shade out all but the shade-tolerant species. Like the annuals, the early woody species are usually those dispersed by light windborne seeds, such as goat, common and eared willows, buddleia and birch. Species with larger seeds but less efficient dispersal, which can colonise urban sites at a later stage, include ash, sycamore, broom, laburnum, rowan, hawthorn, elder, domesticated apple and Swedish whitebeam.

Usually, vacant ground is redeveloped before succession to a **climax community** of mature woodland occurs, so that self-set or partly self-set urban woodland, which often has an unusual mix of wild and introduced species, is a rare wildlife habitat. Disused railway lines and old neglected cemeteries and gardens may provide interesting examples. The progression from bare soil to woodland on an urban site is illustrated in Figure 3.2.

Succession on disturbed ground can be slowed down by stress conditions caused by extremes of pH, reduced availability of nutrients, and drought or waterlogging. This and the variable nature of many sites means that the vegetation cover often remains incomplete or 'open'. Patches of bare ground remain available for further colonisation by new species, and different successional stages occur on the same site, which results in a diverse plant community.

Figure 3.2   Succession from bare soil to woodland on an urban site

Sites with a complete vegetation cover continue to recruit new species, but only very slowly when gaps in the vegetation occur. In intensively managed areas, such as formal parks, sports greens and arable farmland, prevention

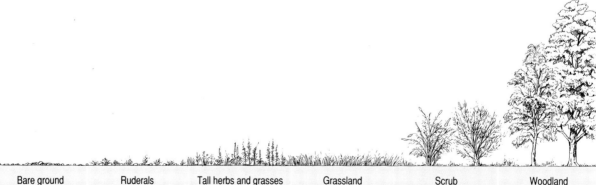

| Bare ground (e.g. demolition site) | Ruderals | Tall herbs and grasses | Grassland | Scrub (e.g. willows, buddleia) | Woodland (e.g. birch, sycamore) |

of colonisation by stray species, and of succession, is normally a management aim, achieved by regular cultivation of flower beds and fields, the use of herbicides and mowing. On some sites, ground cover and the establishment of new species may be suppressed by heavy recreational use, as in some urban woodland.

The animals best adapted to the urban environment are those which are mobile, tolerant of disturbance, and without specialised habitat requirements.

Birds are partly independent of the impact of urbanisation, since they can move relatively easily between sites to find the conditions they need. Those that have successfully adapted to urban living include blackbird, magpie, carrion crow, jay, herring gull and starling. Omnivorous species, such as feral pigeon and house sparrow, predominate in inner city areas, where their natural diet is supplemented, if not almost entirely replaced, by bread and scraps. Insect-eating birds are better represented in the less densely built-up areas and in the larger parks. Among birds of prey, only the kestrel has so far adapted to the inner city, where small birds such as house sparrow replace small mammals as its main food source. Other predators may occur on the urban fringe.

The numbers of birds breeding in urban areas are restricted by the availability of suitable nesting sites and cover. In London, for example, only about 12 species commonly breed in the city centre, compared with 30 in the inner suburbs and more than 80 in parts of the Green Belt. On the other hand, the few species that do breed in inner cities may be present in huge numbers. Tall buildings, especially if they are ornate, with crevices and ledges, may serve in place of cliffs as roosting and nest sites for birds such as kestrel, jackdaw, pigeons (feral rock dove and wood pigeon) and black redstart. Parks and gardens with plenty of shrub and tree cover provide nest sites for birds that are typical of woodland edge habitat, such as blackbird and finches.

Among mammals, fox, grey squirrel, hedgehog and pipistrelle bat have adapted particularly well to urban living. An ability to augment their diet by scavenging and a nocturnal habit are characteristics which help some of these urban mammals to survive. Corridors of semi-natural vegetation, such as railway lines and river banks, may be important in allowing the spread of smaller mammals in built-up areas.

For **invertebrates**, such as insects, spiders, slugs and worms, the isolation of many urban sites may be a barrier to dispersal, especially for those species that are entirely ground-dwelling. The number of different species present tends to decline towards a town or city centre, as shown for **arthropods** (insects, spiders, centipedes and millipedes, crustacea) in Figure 3.3 (overleaf). Strongly flying insects, and money spiders belonging to the Linyphiid family that move by drifting on silken threads, are probably least affected. For insects with more limited powers of flight, such as hoverflies and leaf beetles, gardens can serve as valuable 'stepping stones', allowing dispersal to other sites. However, research using traps placed on rooftops suggests that the barrier effect of the built environment on invertebrate dispersal may have been overemphasised in the past. As with plants, human-mediated dispersal (for example, in mud on the wheels of vehicles) and transport by birds probably play an important part. The presence or absence of invertebrates on a site therefore usually reflects site conditions as much as accessibility.

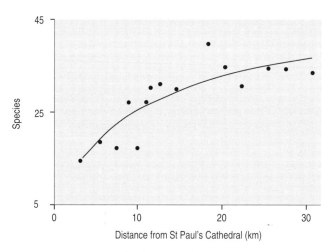

Figure 3.3   Relationship between total arthropod species, identified from 15 London gardens, and distance from the city centre (Source: Davis, 1979, reproduced in Gilbert, 1989)

GULP! — WE'D NEED A HARRIER JUMP JET TO LAND THERE!

Other factors that may adversely affect the distribution of some groups of invertebrates include disturbance from trampling, mowing or cultivation; lack of a layer of leaf litter; limited size or diversity of habitat; and absence of particular **host plants** for breeding and feeding. However, most groups of invertebrates have been little studied. Detailed surveys might reveal that there are many more urban species than are commonly observed, as the two garden surveys previously mentioned suggest. Urban conditions that are likely to attract certain invertebrates include the presence of a great variety of plants that provide nectar and pollen over a prolonged season, warm dry surfaces, refuse dumps, sewage works and areas where food is stored and consumed. Bare ground is particularly valuable for solitary bees and wasps. The early stages of plant succession are good for many uncommon species that disappear as succession proceeds.

3.2   Conducting a wildlife habitat survey

This section describes the procedure for Phase I and Phase II wildlife habitat surveys. Even if your group is mainly interested in a single site, it is useful to be familiar with this systematic approach to site assessment and to complete a standard survey form for your site.

Phase I survey

The Phase I survey is intended to provide an overview and preliminary evaluation of all open space in an area. The survey can be planned by first locating areas of open space by a methodical examination (square by square) of Ordnance Survey maps and recent aerial photographs (usually held by the local authority). A scale of between 1:5000 and 1:12,000 is needed for this purpose, the choice depending on what is available and the density of buildings in the survey area.

Aerial photographs

From aerial photographs it should be possible to distinguish broad habitat types, such as grassland, woodland and arable fields, and to identify sites hidden from view at ground level, for example those surrounded by housing. All the sites should be highlighted on an Ordnance Survey map, with a preliminary indication of their habitat type. Narrow linear features such as roadside verges may not be distinguishable and there may have been changes in the extent of open space since the date of the maps or photographs, so these aspects need checking during ground surveys.

Resources may well limit the extent of ground surveys. If this is the case, the work involved can be limited by restricting the survey area, for example to the inner city or the main built-up area, or by omitting categories of open space that are probably of limited wildlife interest, such as amenity grassland, or by concentrating on the areas that are most susceptible to development or over a certain size. Information on the wildlife interest of some sites may already be available from sources such as local authority planning departments, museums, colleges, wildlife trusts and natural history societies. If so, this can help identify the sites that should definitely be included in the survey. Publicising the survey with the help of the local media may bring to light additional information, for example about privately owned sites.

Ground surveys

In urban areas, ground surveys are better conducted by public transport, by bicycle or on foot rather than by car. A standard survey form should be completed for each site. Large sites can be divided into several more conveniently sized areas for the purpose of the survey, and linear features divided into convenient lengths, with each section being given an individual site code. In the same way, smaller features such as avenues of trees or grass verges can be given a site code if they are to be included in the survey. Private gardens are not usually surveyed, although their total area may be recorded. Other privately owned sites may be included if there is open access, or the vegetation is clearly visible without access, or permission for a survey has been obtained from the owner.

For the ground survey, maps at a scale of 1:2500 or 1:1250 of the area in which the site lies are needed. A scale of 1:10,000 may be adequate for large sites outside the main built-up area. Survey forms are usually based on the one developed for the Leicester habitat survey, shown in Figure 3.4 (overleaf). This can be adapted and simplified if necessary, according to the expertise of the recorders.

Survey forms

At the top of the survey form there is a space for the name of the recorder and the date and time of the survey. The site address, site name or adjacent street name is recorded below. The grid reference (two letters and six numbers) is taken from the Ordnance Survey map, and is based on the approximate position of the centre of the site if the site is large. If the area of the site is unknown it can be estimated later, for example by the 'method of squares' (see Box 3.3 overleaf). Some local authorities have computer facilities to digitise maps and so may be able to provide information on site areas easily. Site ownership is recorded if known.

The nature of the site (for example, cemetery), the dominant types of vegetation and any particularly noticeable features should be recorded in the site description. The space for natural history observations is used to record any obvious or unusual wildlife seen during the site visit, and to note whether or not initial impressions suggest that the site merits a more detailed survey. The boxes for other survey information are ticked once more detailed surveys of any of the major groups of wildlife are completed. The section on site history refers to aspects such as past and existing management and use, and developments planned (P = proposed, O = **outline planning permission**, D = **detailed planning permission**), some of which are discussed more fully in Chapter 4.

LEICESTER HABITAT SURVEY

City Wildlife Project

PARKFIELD
WESTERN PARK
HINCKLEY ROAD
LEICESTER LE3 6HX
TEL: (0533) 856675

NUMBER

NORTH

RECORDER _____ DATE ___ 8 ___ TIME ____ – ____ hrs

SITE ADDRESS _____

GRID REF _____ A – Z REF ____ AREA ____ ha

OWNER _____

TENANT _____

CONDITIONS OF VISIT _____

SITE DESCRIPTION

100m
25m

NATURAL HISTORY OBSERVATIONS

OTHER SURVEY INFORMATION	
Mammals	
Birds	
Reptiles/Amphibs	
Fish	
Butterflies	
Inverts	
Flora	
Fungi	
Ferns	
Mosses	
Lichens	

REMINDER
Boundaries
Adj. land use
Access
Scale
North
Paths
Tipping
Topography

SITE HISTORY

	P	O	D

	Aq – Still	Aq – Flowing	Built	Other	Soil Analysis	Surface Type T C Se S G RA Co	Drainage G M P	Land Use	A a A s A l Ce Ed Ho Sw Ps Rv Rw Wa G R Ti I. C Sp N O

B
C
D
E
F

Figure 3.4   Front and back of Leicester habitat survey form

48

Box 3.3 Estimating the area of a site using the 'method of squares'

In this method, a square grid overlay is placed on an Ordnance Survey map of the site. The size of the grid squares is based on subdivisions of the map's scale, so that the area of each grid square is known. The area of the site is estimated from the number of complete grid squares that lie within the boundary, plus half the number of incomplete squares, multiplied by the area of a single grid square.

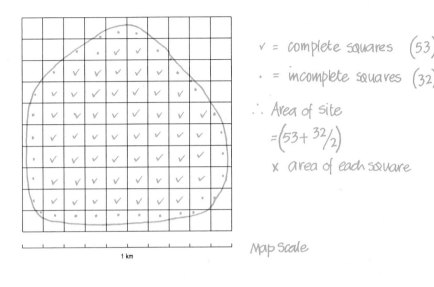

✓ = complete squares (53)

· = incomplete squares (32)

∴ Area of site

$$= \left(53 + \frac{32}{2}\right)$$

× area of each square

1 km — Map Scale

A sketch map of the site should be drawn in the space provided on the reverse of the survey form. The reminder box is a list of points that should be recorded with the sketch, such as an arrow indicating which direction is north. Each distinctive area of the site should be outlined with a dashed line on the sketch. These distinctive areas are termed **parcels** and are labelled alphabetically. For example, a site that has a pond, mown grass and an area of trees has three parcels, which would be labelled A, B and C. Underneath the sketch map is a list of habitat types, land uses and environmental factors; a line should be completed for each parcel, ticking from the list of characteristics shown those that apply to that parcel. The headings and abbreviations used in this list are explained in Table 3.2 overleaf, and an example of a completed survey form is provided in the case study section at the end of this chapter (Figure 3.5).

The information provided from all the site maps is collated on a master map, usually at a scale of 1:10,000. As far as possible within the limitations imposed by this scale, individual parcels are marked on this map. Ideally, a standard range of colours should be used to denote the range of different habitat types (for example, open water is shaded indigo blue and unmanaged grassland orange; a full list of recommended colours is given in the *Handbook for Phase I Habitat Survey*, published by the former Nature Conservancy Council).

Phase II survey

The Phase II survey involves compiling more detailed records of individual sites, and in particular completing a plant species checklist for each parcel on

Table 3.2 Key to headings, abbreviations and codes used on the Leicester habitat survey form

Columns in the table represent habitat types, land uses and environmental factors. For each parcel (lettered on the left hand side) a tick, letter or number indicates these details where present. Where columns offer alternatives e.g. Agriculture/Horticulture, one of the encircled letters is entered in the space below i.e. A or H.

1. *Bareground*: no plants or extremely sparse vegetation.
2. *Agricultural*: where livestock or arable land occur.
   Horticultural: allotments, tree nurseries, garden centres.
3. *Ruderal*: early colonising vegetation such as legumes and crucifers.
4. *Tall herb*: where such plants (e.g. nettles, willowherb), occur as continuous ground cover, but are not dominated by grasses.
5. *Close mown*: grass 10cm high or less.
6. *Occasionally managed*: mown or cut infrequently.
7. *Grazed*: by farm animals or pets including geese. Some areas may be grazed by wild rabbits.
8. *Unmanaged*: grassland areas which may include various herbs and isolated shrubs.
9. *Isolated shrubs*: shrubs or trees less than 8 metres which do not form a continuous canopy.
10. *Scrub*: shrubs and trees (less than 8 metres high) forming a closed canopy. Isolated trees may occur within this habitat.
11. *Hedgerow*: former or remnant hedges may be included if still recognisable as such.
12. *Hedgerow: Continuous/Gappy* - refers to the current state of the hedge, whether an unbroken line or with gaps.
13. *Hedgerow: Layed/Clipped/Unamanged* - refers to the management regime which the hedge has received.

14. *Hedgerow height*: 1, 2, 3, 3+: the height in metres.
15. *Hedgerow survey*: tick if detailed survey information available.
16. *Isolated trees*: greater than 8 metres tall and not forming continuous canopy with other trees.
17. *Woodland*: consists of trees greater than 8 metres tall, forming a closed canopy, which may or may not have a shrub and ground layer.
    Structure: use separate letters (e.g. A, B and C) to denote the different woodland layers (canopy, shrub and ground layers). The same letters must then be used on the corresponding species checklist.
18. *Aquatic marginal*: wetland/marsh habitat. This may include muddy banks which are submerged for only part of the year.
19. *Aquatic still*: ponds, lakes, reservoirs, ditches.
20. *Aquatic flowing*: rivers, streams, canal.
21. *Built*: manmade buildings, structures and artefacts including roads, pylons, foundations, walls, etc.
22. *Other*: any habitat or feature which will not fit easily into one of the above. This should be elaborated in the 'Site Description'.
23. *Soil analysis*: tick if further information is available on file.
24. *Surface type*: note type of substrate including that of aquatic habitats where possible.
    T - Topsoil
    C - Clay
    Se - Sediment
    S - Sand
    G - Gravel
    R - Rubble
    Co - Concrete
    A - Ash
    O - Other
25. *Drainage*: a rating based on a visual appraisal of the site using topography, location, surface type and plant composition as indicators:
    Good: Well drained land, unaffected by waterlogging and lacking any wetland species.
    Moderate: Land subject to occasional waterlogging without the establishment of a wetland flora.
    Poor: land usually by standing or running water, which is subject to flooding and waterlogging. The site will usually support typical wetland plants.
26. *Land use*:
    Aa - Agriculture: arable.
    As - Agriculture: livestock.
    Al - Allotments
    Ce - Cemetery.
    Ed - Educational establishment e.g. schools, colleges
    Ho - Hospital.
    Sw - Sewage works.
    Ps - Public open space: includes public parks and gardens, riverside walks and amenity areas.
    Rv - Road verge.
    Rw - Railway: includes tracks, sidings, cuttings and embankments.
    Wa - Wasteground: areas formerly occupied by buildings, yards etc.
    G - Gardens: private or publicly owned.
    R - Residential: private and council housing.
    Ti - Tip.
    IC - Industrial/commercial premises.
    Sp - Sports-grounds and pitches owned, leased or rented by clubs and societies.
    N - Navigation: where boats and barges use waterways.
    O - Other: where none of the above categories are applicable, give details in the site description.

    Note: Prefix with D if the land use no longer exists.

the site. As for Phase I, a standard survey form should be used, as shown for Reading in the case study section (Figure 3.6). The checklist of plants should be based on a list of all the species that have been recorded locally, with space allowed to add any new ones that may be discovered. It should be possible to obtain such a list from the local biological records office, museum, wildlife trust or natural history society.

To record plant species, a standard procedure should be adopted, for example by surveying **transects** of the same length in each parcel and identifying all the different species seen along the transect. For each parcel, the species present are noted on the checklist either by a tick or by using one of three categories: dominant (d), abundant (a) or rare (r).

If your group is interested mainly in one particular site, or has the time and enthusiasm, members may like to compile additional checklists for other species, such as birds, butterflies or fungi. If your group feels that it lacks the expertise to carry out a detailed plant survey, you could ask for help from a more experienced group, the local authority or a local college, or consider employing a professional ecologist.

A photographic record of the site, including pictures taken from the same vantage points at different times of the year, and of notable species or features, can be useful for monitoring subsequent changes on the site and for preparing publicity and educational materials.

3.3   Exercise 3: Conducting your own wildlife habitat survey

For this exercise you need to select a site to survey. This can be either one with which you are already involved, or a nearby site with public access. You will need a photocopy of an Ordnance Survey map of the area (at a scale of 1:2500 or 1:1250), survey forms based on that shown in Figure 3.4, and a notebook and pen. Binoculars and a camera are useful additional equipment. If you decide to carry out a detailed plant survey, you will also need a plant identification guide and a checklist similar to the one shown in Figure 3.6 in the case study section (but based on a local plant list).

1   Check first whether the wildlife value of the site has already been recognised by statutory or local authority designation (for example, as a Site of Special Scientific Interest or a Local Nature Reserve) and whether any information about the wildlife value of the site already exists.

2   Complete a survey form for the site, including a sketch map showing any distinctive habitat parcels. Mark the site and the parcels on the Ordnance Survey map.

3   If you feel confident about your skill at plant identification, or your ability to use a plant identification guide, complete a checklist of plant species along representative transects of each distinctive parcel on the site. If not, simply record the number of different plants you see along a transect, to give an indication of the plant diversity, without worrying about precise identification.

(If you are carrying out this exercise as part of a group, you might like to survey two sites, so that you can compare them at a later stage.)

3.4   Case study example of a wildlife habitat survey

Reading Urban Wildlife Group and the Reading wildlife habitat survey

Reading Urban Wildlife Group was formed in 1985 in response to a need for greater nature conservation awareness in the urban areas of Reading, especially about planning issues. It soon became apparent to the group that there was a serious lack of detailed information on the wildlife resource of Reading.

The group therefore approached Reading Borough Council who agreed to meet some of the costs and provide maps for a pilot scheme to survey key areas of the borough.

Once this survey was successfully accomplished, the group undertook a survey of the whole area of urban Reading (80 square kilometres) over a period of 3 years. After negotiation, funding was provided by Reading Borough Council, with additional grants from Berkshire County Council, Wokingham District Council and Tilehurst Parish Council. In return, the group agreed to provide a full report of all findings and to allow access to all original documentation. The British Ecological Society provided a start-up grant for the project.

Over 500 sites were surveyed, entirely by volunteer effort. A survey co-ordinator, also a volunteer, was responsible both for personnel and for the collation of documents. Surveyors who became experienced in the first year shared the supervision of less experienced surveyors in the subsequent two years.

The survey was undertaken in two phases. For the Phase I survey, each volunteer was equipped with a 1:1250 map of the locality, coloured pencils, a basic recording card for Phase I information, and a set of notes on a standard procedure for colouring the map according to land use and filling in the boxes on the recording card. The volunteer then walked round likely open spaces, making notes and indicating each habitat type or parcel with different colours on the map. Later a volunteer returned to complete Phase II, recording the species list for each parcel. One of the completed record cards is shown in Figure 3.5 and part of a completed plant checklist for the same site in Figure 3.6.

All information was forwarded to the survey co-ordinator for collation. In due course all the data were analysed using a standard set of criteria and the findings written up as a reference document.

Detailed reports were submitted to the three councils who funded the survey, listing all sites and describing those of particular interest, with reasons. Biological data on sites of interest were copied to the Berkshire, Buckinghamshire and Oxfordshire Naturalist's Trust, to which the group is affiliated. All the information is available to individuals and institutions concerned with planning and nature conservation. A charge for biological data is made to developers.

With hindsight, the Reading Urban Wildlife Group learned several lessons from this massive undertaking. A preliminary examination of aerial photographs to identify sites would have saved volunteers a great deal of leg-work. Some funders wanted immediate information on specific areas that were under threat of development; pressure on volunteers was reduced when these needs were dealt with first, even if it meant laying aside

SITE NAME

NUMBER

SKETCH

NORTH

Allotments

Hedge with mature sycamores

Tall mixed hedge

Houses and gardens

Holly Hedge

Victoria Road — Unmade

Holly Hedge

Scrub

FP

Tall mixed hedge

Houses and gardens

25/50/100m

	Baraground	Agric (Hort)	Ruderal	Tall Herb	Close Mown Grass	Occas. Managed ii	Grazed Grass	Unmanaged Grass	Isol. Shrubs	Scrub	Hedgerow	Cont/Gap	Lay/Clip/Unman	Height 1(2)3 4+	Survey	Isol. Trees	Woodland Structure	Aq – Marginal	Aq – Still	Aq – Flowing	Built	Other	Surface Type	Drainage	Land Use
	1	2	3	4	5	6	7	8	9	10	11	12	13	14 15 16		17	18 19	20	21	22	23	24	25	
A																									
B																									
C																									
D																									
E																									
F																									

PARCELS

READING HABITAT SURVEY

Berks, Bucks & Oxon Naturalists' Trust
Reading Urban Wildlife Group

Please return forms to:-

Bolton Pastures Country Park
Davis St.
Hurst
Reading RG10 0TH

DATE 24.10.85   **RECORDER** LINDA CARTER   **TIME OF VISIT:** 8.45 to 9.15 am

SITE NAME   OLD CEMETERY   **SITE No** 9313

SITE ADDRESS   VICTORIA ROAD,   Grid ref. SU 7 1 5 7 5 7

CAVERSHAM   A-Z ref.   2F

OWNER/TENANT   READING BOROUGH COUNCIL   Area 1.5ha.

ACCESS   [ha/dimensions]

SITE DESCRIPTION including the different parcels identified

This cemetery was opened in 1885, to take the place of St Peters churchyard for burials. It is on the E facing slope of the Ilendean Valley. Some landscaping has been done to level off the ground for graves. The site is now disused, except where there are family plots.

The cemetery was originally planted with a variety of evergreens, such as Douglas Fir, Yew, Cypress, and deciduous trees, surviving are large beeches and round the perimeter a variety of deciduous trees.

A : The surrounding hedge, clipped vertically in places but not topped. This also contains specimen trees.

B : The cemetery grounds, mown 2 or 3 times a year, with predominantly evergreen trees, and a network of tarmaced paths to allow hearses access.

NATURAL HISTORY OBSERVATIONS, eg birds, insects, mammals, and interesting plants

The species of trees are listed on the fieldmap. There is an Acer negundo in poor condition in the S hedge line.

A list of bird species is included. This should not be considered as definitive.

Grey squirrels very active.

OTHER SURVEY INFORMATION	
Mammals	✓
Birds	✓
Reptiles/Ampnibs	
Fish	
Butterflies	✓
Inverts	
Flora	✓
Fungi	
Ferns	
Mosses	
Lichens	

MANAGEMENT/NOTES ON USE, RESTRICTIONS/POTENTIAL/SITUATION/DEVELOPMENTS PLANNED:- preliminary assessment of value

The old timber of the cemetery suffered badly through the Winter of 1981/82 and some of the firs were removed. In 1984 tree surgeons were called in to do general remedial work, such as limb lopping, scrub clearance, etc.

The site is mown 2 or 3 times a year, and is supervised by a retired gravedigger. There is no doubt that this relatively undisturbed site offers good cover for birds as well as foraging territory. Birds are often seen in transit from Balmore Walk on the E flank of the valley to the cemetery on the W.

No flora study could be undertaken at this time.

WORTH FURTHER SURVEY? Yes ✓   Botanical Survey continued 10.6.86
[Species lists]

53

Figure 3.5   Reading habitat survey: example of a completed record card (front and back)

READING HABITAT SURVEY
Berks, Bucks & Oxon Naturalists' Trust
Reading Urban Wildlife Group

SITE NAME: Old Cemetery
SITE Nº: G31 3
GRID REF. SU 7 1 5 7 5 7
RECORDER: Linda Carter
DATE: 10 6 86

A B C D E F TREES & SHRUBS (WOODLAND)

Acer campestre (Field Maple)
Acer platanoides (Norway Maple)
Acer pseudoplatanus (Sycamore)
Aesculus hippocastanum (Horse Chestnut)
Alnus glutinosa (Alder)
Alnus incana (Grey Alder)
Betula pendula (Silver Birch)
Betula pubescens (Downy Birch)
Buddleia davidii (Buddleia)
Carpinus betulus (Hornbeam)
Castanea sativa (Sweet Chestnut)
Chamaecyparis lawsoniana (Lawson's Cypress)
Cornus sanguinea (Dogwood)
Corylus avellana (Hazel)
Cotoneaster sp. (Cotoneaster)
Crataegus laevigata (Midland Hawthorn) — pink
Crataegus monogyna (Hawthorn)
Cytisus scoparius (Broom)
Fagus sylvatica (Common Beech)
Fraxinus excelsior (Ash) — pendula + weeping
Ilex aquifolium (Holly) + hedge
Juglans regia (Walnut)
Laburnum anagyroides (Laburnum)
Larix decidua (European Larch)
Ligustrum ovalifolium (Garden Privet)
Ligustrum vulgare (Wild Privet)
Malus domestica (Cultivated Apple)
Malus sylvestris (Crab Apple)
Picea abies (Norway Spruce)
Pinus sylvestris (Scots Pine)
Platanus hybrida (London Plane)
Populus alba (White Poplar)
Populus x canadensis (Grey Poplar)
Populus nigra v. italica (Lombardy Poplar)
Populus tremula (Aspen)
Prunus sp. (Cherry)
Prunus sp. (Plum)
Prunus spinosa (Blackthorn)
Pyracantha coccinea (Firethorn)
Quercus cerris (Turkey Oak)
Quercus robur (Pedunculate Oak)
Rhamnus catharticus (Buckthorn)
Rhododendron spp. (Rhododendron)
Ribes nigrum (Red Current)
Ribes uva-crispa (Gooseberry)
Robinia pseudoacacia (False Acacia)
Rosa canina (Dog Rose)
Rosa sp. (Rose)
Salix alba (White Willow)
Salix babylonica (Weeping Willow)
Salix caprea (Goat Willow)
Salix cinerea (Grey Willow)
Salix fragilis (Crack Willow)
Salix viminalis (Osier)
Sambucus nigra (Elder)
Sorbus aria (Whitebeam)
Sorbus aucuparia (Rowan)
Taxus baccata (Yew)

b - and many ornamental firs/cypress
Philadelphus

A B C D E F GRASSES, SEDGES & RUSHES

Agropyron caninum (Bearded Couch-grass)
Agropyron repens (Couch-grass)
Agrostis gigantea (Black Bent-grass)
Agrostis stolonifera (Fiorin)
Agrostis tenuis (Common Bent-grass)
Aira caryophyllea (Silver Hair-grass)
Aira praecox (Early Hair-grass)
Alopecurus geniculatus (Marsh Foxtail)
Alopecurus agrourcides (Black Twitch)
Anisantha sterilis (Barren Brome)
Anthoxanthum odoratum (Sweet Vernal-grass)
Arrhenatherum elatius (Oat-grass)
Avena fatua (Wild Oat)
Brachypodium sylvaticum (Slender False-Brome)
Briza media (Quaking-grass)
Bromus mollis (Lop-grass)
Carex flacca (Carnation-grass)
Carex hirta (Hammer Sedge)
Carex ovalis (False Fox-Sedge)
Carex riparia (Great Pond Sedge)
Catapodium rigidum (Hard Poa)
Cynosurus cristatus (Crested Dog's Tail)
Dactylis glomerata (Cock's-foot)
Deschampsia caespitosa (Tufted Hairgrass)
Festuca arundinacea (Tall Fescue)
Festuca gigantea (Tall Brome)
Festuca pratensis (Meadow Fescue)
Festuca rubra (Red Fescue)
Glyceria fluitans (Floto-grass)
Glyceria maxima (Reed-grass)
Holcus lanatus (Yorkshire Fog)
Holcus mollis (Creeping Soft-grass)
Hordeum murinum (Wall Barley)
Hordeum secalinum (Meadow Barley)
Juncus articulatus (Jointed Rush)
Juncus bufonius (Toad Rush)
Juncus conglomeratus (Conglomerate Rush)
Juncus effusus (Soft Rush)
Juncus inflexus (Hard Rush)
Lolium perenne (Rye-grass)
Luzula campestris (Field Woodrush)
Melica uniflora (Wood Melick)
Phalaris arundinacea (Reed-grass)
Phleum bertolonii (Cat's Tail)
Phleum pratense (Timothy)
Phragmites australis (Reed)
Poa annua (Annual Poa)
Poa pratensis (Smooth-stalked Mdw.)
Poa trivialis (Rough-stalked Mdw.)
Scirpus lacustris (Bulrush)
Trisetum flavescens (Yellow Oat)
Typha latifolia (Great Reedmace)
Vulpia bromoides (Barren Fescue)

A B C D E F TREES & SHRUBS (WOODLAND)

Tilia x vulgaris (Common Lime)
Ulex europaeus (Gorse)
Ulmus procera (English Elm)
Viburnum opulus (Guelder Rose)
Cotoneaster *horizontalis?*
Buxus semper virens
Lonicera *periclymenum? Pubescens*

A B C D E F GRASSES, SEDGES & RUSHES

Vulpia myuros (Rat's Tail Fescue)
Zerna ramosa (Hairy Brome)
Bromus sterilis
Festuca ovina
Festuca rubra

A B C D E F HERBS

Achillea millefolium (Yarrow)
Acorus calamus (Sweet Flag)
Aegopodium podagraria (Ground Elder)
Aethusa cynapium (Fool's Parsley)
Alisma plantago-aquatica (Common W. Plantain)
Alliaria petiolata (Garlic Mustard)
Anagallis arvensis (Scarlet Pimpernel)
Anemone nemorosa (Wood Anemone)
Angelica archangelica (Garden Angelica)
Angelica sylvestris (Angelica)
Antennaria dioica (Soapdragon)
Antirrhinum majus (Snapdragon)
Apium nodiflorum (Fool's Watercress)
Arabidopsis thaliana (Thale Cress)
Arctium minus (Lesser Burdock)
Armoracia rusticana (Horseradish)
Artemisia absinthium (Wormwood)
Artemisia vulgaris (Mugwort)
Arum maculatum (Lords and Ladies)
Aster novi-belgii (Michaelmas Daisy)
Atriplex hastata (Marsh Orache)
Atriplex patula (Common Orache)
Atropa bella-donna (Deadly Nightshade)
Ballota nigra (Black Horehound)
Barbarea stricta (Sm. Fl. Wintercress)
Barbarea vulgaris (Common Wintercress)
Bellis perennis (Daisy)
Berula erecta (Lesser Water Parsnip)
Brassica napus (Rape)
Bryonia cretica (White Bryony)
Callitriche stagnalis (Starwort)
Caltha palustris (Marsh Marigold)
Calystegia sepium (Hedge Bindweed)
Calystegia silvatica (Great Bindweed)
Capsella bursa-pastoris (Shepherd's Purse)
Cardamine amara (Large Bittercress)
Cardamine flexuosa (Wavy Bittercress)
Cardamine hirsuta (Hairy Bittercress)
Cardamine pratensis (Cuckoo Flower)
Cardaria draba (Hoary Cress)
Carduus acanthoides (Welted Thistle)
Carduus nutans (Musk Thistle)
Centaurea nigra (Black Knapweed)
Cerastium fontanum (Mouse Ear)
Cerastium glomeratum (Sticky Mouse Ear)
Chaenorhinum minus (Small Toadflax)
Chamomilla suaveolens (Pineapple Mayweed)
Chamomilla recutita (Scented Mayweed)
Chelidonium majus (Greater Celandine)
Chenopodium album (Fat Hen)
Chenopodium bonus-henricus (Good King Henry)
Chenopodium rubrum (Red Goosefoot)
Circaea lutetiana (Enchanter's Nightshade)
Cirsium arvense (Creeping Thistle)

Figure 3.6 Reading habitat survey: example of part of a completed plant checklist

geographically logical progress for a while. Volunteers needed regular support from someone they considered to be 'an authority'; one-to-one discussions often worked better than large meetings. Covering the whole area of Reading was daunting; volunteers would have preferred to target specific sites in turn, such as cemeteries or old woodland, rather than cover the whole area in geographical progression.

The importance of not simply recording information, but of analysing it and disseminating it to authorities with planning powers has been underlined by the progress that has been made since the survey was completed. Partly as a result of the survey, a Nature Conservation Forum for Berkshire has been set up and has produced a detailed nature conservation strategy. This has a complete section devoted to urban nature conservation. Urban wildlife sites are now offered some measure of protection in the structure plan for Berkshire and the local plans for each district, by designation as **Wildlife Heritage Sites**. The survey data are fully used in responses to planning applications. Local councils are selecting the key sites for designation as Local Nature Reserves.

(Source: Linda Carter, Reading Urban Wildlife Group)

Chapter 4

ASSESSING SITES FOR THEIR VALUE TO THE COMMUNITY

To complete your assessment of urban sites, you need to record information about the wider value of a site to the community, over and above its wildlife value, and about any restrictions that may limit a site's use as a wildlife area for the community. The detailed knowledge that local people often have or can obtain of sites in their own neighbourhood is invaluable for this part of the survey, and not easily matched by officials with responsibility for a larger area. This type of information can play a significant part in planning decisions about a site, as it did in the case of Royate Hill Embankment and Forest Lane Park mentioned in Chapter 2.

For an area-wide survey, basic information on characteristics relating to a site's wider value is usually collected at the time of the Phase I and Phase II surveys and recorded on the same survey form. However, if your group plans to be involved with the management or use of the site you are surveying, you will probably want to compile a more detailed record. This additional information can be recorded on separate pages and filed with the survey form. You may prefer to gather some of the information, such as that about the site's historical background, over an extended period, provided it does not affect the site's management and there is no pressure to supply it quickly to safeguard the site or to secure funding.

This chapter discusses the main factors that need to be considered in assessing a site's value to the community. It describes how these can be used as criteria, in conjunction with the wildlife criteria, for selecting sites to be retained or developed as wildlife areas and subsequently for guiding the choice of appropriate management options to meet the objectives agreed for a site. The chapter includes an exercise on the assessment of the wider community aspects of a site for you to carry out, and a case study example describing the assessment of sites in Dundee.

4.1 Factors influencing a site's value to the community

In the selection of urban sites to be maintained or developed as wildlife areas it is not just their wildlife interest that needs to be considered. Many other aspects may affect the value of a site to the community. Some are social, relating to people's perception of the site, and others are physical, influencing their actions. Apart from the wildlife interest of a site, the main points to consider are:

▶ access and accessibility;

▶ form of ownership;

▶ community interest and involvement;

▶ historical and cultural significance;

▶ landscape value and aesthetic appeal;

▶ size.

Other factors that may affect the selection of a site as a wildlife area include whether or not it poses any hazards to visitors, the presence of any underground obstructions such as gas pipes, electricity cables and sewers, and the resources that are likely to be needed for site development and maintenance. In a detailed analysis, planners might need to consider the contribution of a site to environmental quality, in terms of such things as groundwater recharge and absorption of pollutants.

Access and accessibility

In urban areas it is important that wildlife areas should be enjoyed by as many people as possible. From this point of view, sites on publicly owned land where there is free access are therefore ideal.

Sites will be of most benefit to a community if they are situated in densely populated areas, and within easy walking distance of local schools (preferably without any intervening major roads). Sites that are overlooked by houses or offices provide an interesting view for those living and working nearby and are less likely to suffer from vandalism.

Accessibility for children in pushchairs and older people or people with disabilities needs to be considered. Although there are measures that can be taken within a site to improve access for less mobile people, such as creating appropriate paths and building raised beds, sites on steep slopes or those that are cold and overshadowed may exclude older or very young visitors.

If there are parts of a site that could be damaged by disturbance or extensive use, they will need to be protected, for example by routing paths away from them or screening them with thickets of scrub. On small community owned or run sites, access may need to be limited, perhaps by restricting opening hours to times when there is a warden present, or by using a keyholder system.

Form of ownership

Ownership of sites by a conservation group or a local authority provides some protection from development pressures and should be the aim for wildlife sites of outstanding importance to a town or city. If a wildlife site of considerable significance to the whole community is not publicly owned, it may be possible to convince the local authority to buy it on the community's behalf, as happened in the case of Plants Brook Local Nature Reserve in Birmingham.

Public and private landowners may be willing to let vacant land (sometimes for a nominal, or **peppercorn**, rent) or release it under **licence** for use as a nature reserve. In this case, information about the conditions and likely length of tenure are needed. A site may be designated for eventual change of use in local plans, or it may have outline or detailed planning permission. Sites with detailed planning permission have to be developed within five years if the permission is not to lapse, so that nature reserves on such sites can only be temporary unless the developer is prepared to incorporate at least part of the reserve into the eventual landscaping of the site. A long lease allows long-term planning and makes investment in terms of resources and effort more worthwhile, as well as allowing more time for the wildlife interest of a site to develop. A licence is the least secure and least satisfactory option, allowing only limited rights to the use of a site for a stated period of time. The licencee has no legal protection except the right to reasonable notice.

If your group is considering renting a site or managing it under a licence, it is important to seek legal advice before signing an agreement with the landowner, whether public or private. The question of who is liable for the cost of any damage should an accident occur, for example if a tree is felled across a neighbouring garden, should be clearly defined.

It is not always easy to track down the existing ownership of sites, although there are several sources of information that can be consulted. Borough and district councils keep records of vacant land for a vacant land register held by the Department of the Environment (or the Scottish Office, in Scotland). All public landowners must register their land holdings in Her Majesty's Land Register; this applies for example to land owned by British Waterways, the British Railways Property Board and all borough, metropolitan and county councils. Directories such as Kelly's Directory, which were produced annually for many towns and cities until the 1970s, give details of the occupiers of businesses and residential properties street by street up to that time. Neighbouring property owners may be able to provide additional information about the ownership of adjoining land.

Community interest and involvement

Local interest in a site and the willingness of local volunteers to help look after a site can be key deciding factors in site selection. Assessment of the social value of a site should therefore take account of existing levels of use (presuming that the site is already accessible) and of any groups or sections of the community that are, or would like to be, involved in its management.

Existing levels of use can be assessed by noting the presence of well-worn tracks, or the number of people using the site while the survey is in progress. If the resources and time are available, more extensive observations of use can be made, for example by recording the number of people who use the site over a specified period (during weekdays as well as weekends), and noting such characteristics as their age and how they use the site (for example, exercising a dog, relaxing in the sun, climbing trees). A potential wildlife area may already have been unofficially adopted, for example as a meeting place for local teenagers; if so, this use should be noted since it may need to be accommodated in any plans, or alternative sites considered.

Where a new site is to be developed as a wildlife area, it is essential to have local approval, if not practical support, if it is to be successful. Public meetings can be used to determine how local people, and adjacent landowners and neighbours, would prefer a site to be managed and what type of facilities they would like to see incorporated; for example, a children's play area, a scented garden or a school study centre. Visual aids, such as sketches or even three-dimensional models, can help stimulate public debate about proposals.

Historical and cultural significance

Some urban sites have a long and interesting history. For example, sites that were once intensively managed but have since been neglected, such as Victorian cemeteries and the grounds of large old houses, may contain interesting cultivated plants that were fashionable or recently introduced at the time they were originally laid out. As already mentioned, derelict industrial sites may have unusual plants that were originally brought in with the raw materials used in the industry or that flourish in the conditions created by the waste. Such features add to a site's interest and so need to be conserved and their origin recorded.

A site may have important cultural associations that should be taken into account in management proposals, since they help preserve the distinctive identity of a neighbourhood and encourage a sense of community pride. For example, in Middleton, Great Manchester where the Groundwork Trust have created a natural landscape on the site of an old dyeworks and neglected army drill hut, the terracotta tiles depicting the emblems of the troops who once used the hut have been rescued and incorporated into a wall surrounding the site. On a site in Liverpool's docklands, large anchors have been used as a landscape feature, serving as a climbing frame for children and a link with the site's past.

Information about a site's history can be obtained from sources such as the local library or museum, the local history society, and the district, borough or county council records office. Useful sources of information include old maps, company records, and old photographs (including aerial photographs). The personal accounts of local people can provide valuable additional information; old maps and photographs can serve as an excellent trigger for their reminiscences.

Landscape value and aesthetic appeal

Many urban sites that are of wildlife importance are of considerable landscape significance too, especially those that cover a large area or that can be seen from a distance. Smaller sites with less visual impact may nevertheless be important locally, providing a pleasant contrast with the built environment and helping to screen unsightly areas from view. Open areas of semi-natural vegetation may make an important contribution to the character of a town or city, particularly where they lie near approach roads or alongside major through routes.

Individual trees or small groups of trees may be protected from removal by **Tree Preservation Orders** (TPOs) if they are a significant landscape feature. Some local authorities give their own planning designation to areas they consider to be of particular landscape significance. In London, for example, these are called **Areas of Special Character**; they include both built and natural landscapes, especially those which contribute a distinctive skyline.

Some types of wildlife habitat may have wider aesthetic appeal than others. For example, people may prefer woodland to marshes, or wildflower meadows to the rough grassland that benefits many insects. This may influence both the selection of sites and their management. Important wildlife habitats with less obvious visual appeal may need extra effort devoted to publicising why they are considered to be of wildlife significance.

In planning the management of a new wildlife area, it is important to seek out and consider the opinions of those most affected by the view. Some people may dislike the appearance of wild areas and feel that they look unkempt. A simple compromise in this case is to ensure that the edges of a site are kept tidy, for example by regularly clearing litter, keeping the border well trimmed and planting attractive flowering and berry-bearing shrubs. New sites should be designed in such a way that they always add to, rather than detract from, the appearance of a neighbourhood.

Size

The size of a site has an important bearing on its value for wildlife but may also have other implications. In general, the management of a single large site will be less costly than that of several small sites covering an equivalent area. This may influence the selection of sites by a local authority or large

QUICK, HIDE! IT'S THOSE KIDS FROM THE NURSERY SCHOOL AGAIN...

voluntary conservation group, although community groups may prefer a small site that is more easily managed.

A site that is to be used regularly for educational purposes and school visits needs to be large enough or resilient enough to absorb the pressure of many pairs of feet and frequent wildlife sampling. A large site can be zoned so that only a proportion is accessible at any one time, while the rest of the site is protected from disturbance. If small sites are to be used to create nature reserves they need to be planned to withstand visitor pressure, or the number of visitors needs to be limited. Camley Street Natural Park, near King's Cross Station in London, is only 0.9 hectares and yet is visited by 10,000 schoolchildren a year, showing that with careful planning a small site can be heavily used and still retain wildlife interest. In the London Borough of Southwark a tiny pond, 4 square metres in area, is managed as a nature reserve by the London Wildlife Trust with the help of a school nature club; access is by arrangement with the Trust.

Hazards to visitors

Assessment of a site should include a note of any potential hazards such as toxic waste, old mine shafts, rusting machinery, unstable slopes, cliffs or deep water. Whilst excessive attention to safety is likely to interfere with the natural appeal of a wild site, precautions should be taken to minimise any risks to visitors, especially on sites used by young children. For example, potentially hazardous areas can be made inaccessible by dense screens of thorny shrubs, and accessible points at the edge of ponds and lakes can be gently shelved. Sites where the public need to be protected from hazards are likely to involve additional management costs.

Presence of underground obstructions

A record of the position of any underground obstructions such as gas pipes, electricity cables, sewers, the foundations of old buildings, and tunnels will be needed if any major earthworks, such as pond creation, are planned. Details of the position of underground services should be available from the site's owner, or the local offices of the service concerned.

Resources

If sites are to be selected for development as community nature reserves, a rough estimate of the resources likely to be involved in establishing and managing the site will be needed. Greater costs are associated with landscaping a new site to simulate natural habitats than with retaining existing vegetation cover. However, sites where management intervention is minimal may require greater investment in interpretation and wardening. A checklist of possible costs is shown in Table 4.1. The Groundwork Trust have developed a computer-based system for landscape management that can provide an estimate of maintenance costs according to a site's size and design.

4.2   Site evaluation

As mentioned in the case study of the Reading wildlife habitat survey, if you take part in an area-wide survey it is very important to analyse the information you gather and present it in a form that can be used by planners.

60

Table 4.1 Checklist of possible costs for establishing and running a nature area

Capital	Revenue
Site clearance and preparation drainage, soil capping)	Staff salaries (staff expenses and training)
Landscaping	Running costs of buildings (water, electricity, gas)
Fencing	Maintenance costs of buildings and other structures
Buildings and services (telephone, water, sewerage, electricity, gas)	Tools
Other structures (jetties, platforms, boardwalks, footpaths, gates, pond liners, steps)	Plant material
Signs	Stationery and photocopying
Materials (tools)	Insurance
Contractors' and professional fees	Security
Machinery hire	Postage
	Telephone
	Events
	Publications
	Publicity
	Annual rental (lease or licence)

(Source: London Ecology Unit, 1990)

For this purpose, the survey information can be used to grade sites into categories, for example excellent, good, moderate and poor, according to their wildlife and social value, on the basis of selected criteria.

The criteria most often used for evaluating urban wildlife sites are:

▶ species or habitat diversity;

▶ species or habitat rarity;

▶ site size;

▶ continuity or permanence of management;

▶ level of community use and involvement;

▶ educational value.

Applying the criteria to the evaluation of a range of sites in a particular town or city is essentially a subjective exercise. No hard-and-fast rules apply and even the opinions of experts are likely to differ to some extent. Judgements are best made in a local context rather than by attempting to standardise criteria for all urban areas country-wide, or even throughout a conurbation.

The main point is to make sure that the criteria used in any evaluation are clearly described in the survey report so that other people have the opportunity to check, and if necessary reassess, the decision. A good example is provided by the case study at the end of this chapter.

Each site can be rated, using a maximum of three or four points for each criterion. More complex systems of scoring are likely to give a false sense of precision. The following examples are intended only as a guide; they should be adapted to suit your purpose and location. They can be tested on local sites that have already been judged by experts to be of good, moderate or poor wildlife value, to check that they give sensible results before they are widely applied.

Diversity

A score for diversity can be based either on the number of different habitat types present on a site, or on the number of different plant species if a detailed survey has been done. For species diversity, a three or four point scale can be devised on the basis of the minimum, average and maximum number of species recorded across all sites surveyed. However, keep in mind that some valuable habitats are species-poor and that evaluation based on diversity tends to favour sites that provide habitat for generalist rather than specialist species.

Rarity

A score for rarity can be based on the number of sites where a species or habitat is present in the survey area, adjusted if appropriate to take account of the distance to the next known occurrence outside the area.

Size

The scale for scoring size needs to be related to the relative abundance of sites in the area. For example, in areas with little open space, sites of less than 0.5 hectares might score one point, those from 0.5 to 1 hectares two points, and those of more than 1 hectare three points. In areas with more open space, broader size categories might be used.

Permanence

The scoring for permanence could be based on the length of time that an area of semi-natural vegetation has been left, or encouraged, to develop. As an example, areas of semi-natural vegetation that have been present more than 50 years could score three, from 10 to 50 years score two, from 5 to 10 years score one, and less than 5 years score zero. The security of the site from development and change in the future might also be taken into account in the score. In using this criterion, keep in mind that sites in the early stages of succession provide habitat for ruderals and invertebrate specialists, which include many of the rarities associated with urban sites. Therefore, even though a site fails to score on the criterion of permanence, it may nevertheless still have a considerable value as a wildlife habitat.

Community use

A score for community use could be based on the numbers of people using the site during the survey, compared with minimum, mean and maximum numbers recorded on all other sites. An additional point could be awarded if it is known that there is a commitment among the local community to retaining or developing a site as a wildlife area.

Educational value

A score for educational value could be based mainly on the number of schools within easy reach of a site. Other aspects that might affect a site's educational value, such as habitat diversity and size, would be already covered by the other criteria.

Since the separate scales are not comparable, it is generally better to consider scores for each criterion in parallel rather than to add them together. Site evaluation can be used both to identify key sites for planning purposes and, if your group would like to become involved in a site's use and management, to decide whether or not a particular site meets your needs. For example, if your group would like to adopt a site as a school nature study area, and has a choice of two sites, your main criteria might be proximity to schools, and the diversity of habitats that exist or could be created with the resources that are likely to be available.

For planning purposes, you might decide, for example, that a site that scored at least two for three of the wildlife criteria, and at least one for one of the social criteria, should be designated a site of high value.

4.3   Translating site evaluation into effective policies

Once sites have been categorised, each category can be made the subject of a particular planning policy. For example, for its most important wildlife sites, Leicester City Council has the following policy statement in its *Ecology Strategy* document: 'The City Council will take appropriate steps to safeguard sites or features of city-wide (A* grade) and local (A grade) ecological importance ... and will not normally permit development on, or close enough to adversely affect, such sites.'

The names given to the different categories vary widely among local authorities, but in general they distinguish between three main types of wildlife site:

▶ sites of significant wildlife interest;

▶ sites of lesser wildlife interest but of significant value to the local community;

▶ green 'corridors', such as rivers and railway lines, which facilitate the movement of wildlife into and through built-up areas.

In addition, local authorities may distinguish **areas of deficiency**: built-up areas where people have no wild open space within easy reach. In these areas, their policy is to look for opportunities to create wildlife areas.

Policies and proposals about each type of site can be incorporated into local plans, which, once adopted by councillors and approved by the Department of the Environment, can be used to guide decisions about individual planning applications. Alternatively, the local authority may publish its proposals in detail as a separate document such as a nature conservation strategy, environmental charter or green plan. Such documents can also be used to inform planning decisions, provided they have been adopted by the full council after public consultation. Local authorities can strengthen the protection they provide for key wildlife sites on land that they own or control by designating them as Local Nature Reserves, as noted already in Table 2.2. They may encourage the implementation of their nature conservation strategy by targeting a particular project area, for example along a river corridor, and offering grants, advice and materials to develop the wildlife and amenity interest of sites within that area.

4.4 Exercise 4: Carrying out your own assessment of the wider value of a site to the community

This exercise should be completed for the same site (or sites) that you surveyed for Exercise 3, using the same survey form. If there is insufficient space for the additional information on the form, record it on separate sheets of paper, identifying the name of the site at the top of each page.

1 On the survey form, record whether the access is open or restricted. On the sketch map, mark any tracks and footpaths, and indicate the type of boundary, noting, if relevant, its state of repair. Add under the site description your comments about the site's accessibility, proximity to schools and apparent level of use by the community.

2 If you consider a site, or any feature on it (such as a specimen tree), is of significant landscape value make a note of this, giving your reasons, under the site description. The position of landscape features should be marked on the sketch map. (Photographs or sketches will add to your record.) Any landscape designation that applies to the site should also be recorded.

3 Record any obvious hazards or obstructions.

4 If you have time, find out and record as much information as you can about the site's ownership, history and community involvement.

(If you have surveyed two sites, as part of a group exercise, you can compare them by adapting the approach described in Section 4.2 or the simpler version described in the following case study example.)

4.5 Case study example of the assessment of sites, including their community value

Evaluation of green space in Dundee

The evaluation of Dundee's green space has been chosen as an example because the survey report contains a very clear explanation of how key sites were selected. The amenity and educational values of sites were important selection criteria and were considered alongside wildlife criteria. The survey form used to record information about sites was similar to the one used for the Reading survey, but there are many differences between the two surveys that help illustrate the variations in approach that occur.

The Dundee survey was initiated and funded jointly by the City of Dundee District Council and the former Nature Conservancy Council. An urban wildlife project was established and a salaried project officer appointed to undertake the survey, with support from various council departments, the Dundee Naturalists' Society and the Dundee Tree Group.

As resources were limited, sources of information that were already available were used to identify the sites most worthy of survey. These sources included the Derelict Land Register, staff in the district council's parks department, the Natural History Museum, the countryside rangers and members of groups such as the Dundee Tree Group and the Dundee Naturalists' Society. Survey forms and detailed plant lists were completed for a total of 47 sites. A sample survey form is shown in Figure 4.1 (overleaf). (Note that the list of habitat types is simpler than that on the Reading survey form, and that shading rather than colour has been used to identify different habitat parcels on the sketch map.)

The importance of each site was evaluated according to the following criteria.

The amenity value was based on the uses of the site at the time of surveying. A point was allocated to the site on this criterion if it was apparent that people were frequently using the site. Indications used were: the presence of paths trodden in the vegetation; the presence of children's dens; people walking on the the site or exercising their dogs while the surveyor was there.

Amenity value

A point was allocated for educational value if the site was within easy walking distance of a school or other educational establishment. Account was taken of whether schools were primary or secondary as secondary schoolchildren would be able to travel longer distances.

Educational value

A site was allocated a point for species diversity if it contained 36 or more species of plant. This number was chosen because it was the average number of species found per site.

Species diversity

The majority of sites surveyed contained only one or two different habitat types. For this reason, sites with three different habitat types were allocated a point on this criterion.

Habitat diversity

Certain habitat types, such as hedgerows, woodland and aquatic habitats, are rare in the city and so were awarded a point.

Habitat rarity

Habitats were divided into three groups of sizes: less than 0.5 hectares (the smallest site surveyed was 0.045 hectares); from 0.5 to less than 1.0 hectares; from 1.0 hectares upwards. Between one and three points were awarded, according to size.

Size

The results of the evaluation are shown in Table 4.2 (overleaf) for some of the sites. The final allocation of points amounted to a maximum of eight points. On the basis of point-allocation sites were divided into four categories: Category A where the score was 7–8; Category B where the score was 5–6; Category C where the score was 3–4; and Category D where the score was 1–2.

The survey report gave the following general descriptions and recommendations about the different categories of sites.

Category A sites are the best in the city. They are already of importance both to the community and to wildlife within the city. These are the most diverse, unusual habitats, which are generally in excellent condition. It is important that these sites are protected from development and that they are actively managed to maintain and enhance their wildlife value as well as possibly improve their interpretative potential to the surrounding population.

Category B sites have considerable potential for amenity or education and wildlife purposes. They do, however, require some positive management to bring them up to a standard equivalent to Category A. The work necessary to improve their scoring differs for each site; for some it would require only some diversification of the flora but for others a whole change in the management regime would be needed.

SITE: DISUSED QUARRY, DERWENT AVENUE

KEY:
- Scrub   --- Path
- Woodland   S = soil
- Managed grassland

HOUSING

DUNMORE STREET

DUNMORE AVENUE

DERWENT AVENUE

ASHMORE STREET

HOUSING

	BAREGROUND	AGRIC/HORT	SHORT HERB	TALL HERB	GRASSLAND				ISOL.SHRUB	SCRUB	HEDGEROW	ISOL.TREE	WOODLAND	AQUATIC				BUILT	SURFACE TYPE
					SHORT Unmanaged	TALL Unmanaged	SHORT Managed	TALL Managed						MARGINAL	STILL	FLOWING			
A				✓		✓													S
B												✓	✓						S
C							✓													S
D																			
E																			

Site   :   Disused Quarry, Derwent Avenue

Reference Number :   4

O.S. Reference   :   3933 NW

Area   :   0.75 ha

Owner   :   Dundee District Council

Access   :   Access is via Derwent Avenue where a well worn path
                    over the grass (c) leads to a path over the main
                    quarry area. Access from Dunmore Street is
                    possible through a break in the chain-link fence.

Site Description :   This quarry has been out of use for a number of years
                    allowing the vegetation to regenerate naturally.
                    The site is a small hill with steep slopes up to
                    the smaller Area C where it reaches its peak. The
                    path near this point is severely eroded, exposing
                    the underlying rock.   There has been an attempt to
                    stop this erosion by erecting a barrier of scaffolding,
                    however this seems to act as a support helping people
                    to negotiate the path.   The site is surrounded by
                    housing and is used as a short cut and play area.

                    The site divides into three different habitats. Areas
                    marked C are planted with amenity grassland which is
                    kept mown. The large Area C on the corner of Derwent
                    Avenue and Ashmore Street contains a solitary, mature
                    silver birch (Betula pendula).

                    Area B is a wooded area with the dominant tree Ash
                    (Fraxinus excelsior) and an understorey of Elder
                    (Sambucus nigra). This combination tended to shade
                    out the herb layer which was very sparse and
                    consisted almost solely of Yorkshire Fog (Holcus
                    lanatus).

                    The main area (A) was dominated by Broom (Cytisus
                    scoparius) although other shrubs were present such
                    as Gorse (Ulex europaeus) and Hawthorn (Crataegus
                    monogyna). Tall, lank grasses such as Common Bent
                    (Agrostis tenuis) dominated the herb layer.
                    Associated with this grassland were species like
                    Field Scabious (Knautia arvensis) and Lady's Bedstraw
                    (Galium verum).

                    There was no sign of dumping on any of the site.

Figure 4.1   Completed survey form (front and back) for a site in Dundee

Table 4.2 Evaluation of some of the 47 green space sites surveyed in Dundee

Ref. no.	Site	Amenity value	Educational value	Species diversity	Habitat diversity	Habitat rarity	Size	Total	Category
1	Dickson Avenue	1	1	1	1	1	3	8	A
2	Glamis Road	1	1	1	–	–	3	6	B
3	Broughty Ferry Road	1	–	–	–	–	1	2	D
4	Derwent Avenue	1	1	1	1	1	2	7	A
5	Law Crescent						2	2	D
6	East Dock Street						2	2	D
7	St Leonard Place	1	1			1	3	6	B
8	Buttars Loan	1				1	1	3	C
9	Donald's Lane						2	2	D
10	Mains Road/Mid Road	1		1	1		2	5	B
11	20 Roseangle	1		1		1	1	4	C
12	Roseangle			1	1	1	2	5	B
13	Constable Street						2	2	D
14	Princes Street	1		1	1	1	1	5	B
15	The Law	1		1	1	1	3	7	A
16	Mid Road						1	1	D
17	Colan Road	1	1	1		1	1	5	B
18	Graham Place	1					1	2	D
19	Robertson Street	1					1	2	D
20	Fairfield Street/Old Glamis Road						1	1	D
21	Fairmuir Road/Old Glamis Road	1					1	2	D
22	Constitution Street /Hilltown	1					1	2	D
23	North George Street /Hilltown	1					1	2	D
24	Catherine Street	1	1				1	3	C
25	Arran Drive	1	1				1	3	C

(Source: Nature Conservancy Council *et al.*, 1988)

Category C sites have poor diversity, tend to be rather small and not of much value to the surrounding community. They could eventually be of some value to the community and wildlife but would require some intensive work. Most of these sites are considered an 'eyesore' by the public and some work to improve their interest would be valuable. Some parks fall into this category, only scoring on amenity value and size.

Category D sites are very poor in terms of both community use and wildlife. Should development take place the only loss would be the loss of open space, rather than anything existing on the site.

The survey report recommended that sites in Categories A and B, only 34% of all sites surveyed, should be retained as open space. It noted that the distribution of these sites is uneven and that some modern housing estates, although containing amenity grassland areas, do not have sites of any value to wildlife. It recommended that these areas should be seen as a priority for developing some wildlife interest. The importance to wildlife of the two main linear features, the Dighty (a burn or stream) and the railway line, was stressed.

(Source: Nature Conservancy Council *et al.*, 1988)

Chapter 5

MAINTAINING AND ENHANCING EXISTING HABITATS

Once you have a detailed record of the existing value of a site, a clear set of objectives for its use, and a knowledge of any constraints that are likely to apply, you have a very good basis for deciding the most appropriate form of management in future. This stage, involving the production of a management plan for individual sites, is sometimes referred to as a **Phase III survey**.

In terms of wildlife conservation, the main objectives of management should be:

1   to *retain* the value of habitats that already have a high wildlife value, by maintaining the conditions that have contributed to their present interest as far as possible;

2   to *enhance* the value of habitats of moderate wildlife value, by increasing diversity or by encouraging particular species;

3   to *create* new wildlife habitats in areas with little existing wildlife value.

This chapter describes the principal options available for maintaining and enhancing the three types of wildlife habitat most commonly found on urban sites: grassland, woodland and aquatic habitats. The options for grassland include the management of tall herb communities that are common on waste ground; the options for woodland include the management of scrub, hedgerows and small groups of trees; and the options for aquatic habitats include the management of small lakes, ponds, streams and ditches. Only the main points are discussed here; further information about habitat management can be found in the other books in the *Practical Conservation* series and in the publications listed in Appendix I. If you would like to try and encourage particular species on a site, you need to know exactly the habitat conditions they require; detailed advice of this kind is available from specialist wildlife societies, such as the British Butterfly Conservation Society and the British Herpetological Society, which are listed in the *Helpful Organisations* supplementary booklet with the foundation book. Options for creating new areas of wildlife habitat are described in Chapter 6.

If you are uncertain about the best way to manage an area which you consider to be of high wildlife value, it is important to seek expert advice, for example from the local wildlife trust or urban wildlife group. In the case of Sites of Special Scientific Interest, there is a legal obligation to consult English Nature, the Countryside Council for Wales or Scottish Natural Heritage before altering the management of a site in a way that might damage its original interest; the owner of the land will hold a list of operations requiring consultation.

5.1   General management considerations

Objectives and constraints

Urban sites usually have to fulfil a variety of objectives. A well thought out management plan can help ensure that as many objectives as possible are met. Objectives can usually be ordered into three levels, according to how specific they are. At the top level are strategic objectives, which tend to be

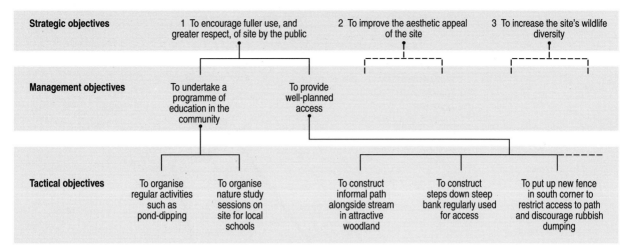

| Strategic objectives | 1 To encourage fuller use, and greater respect, of site by the public | | 2 To improve the aesthetic appeal of the site | 3 To increase the site's wildlife diversity |

| Management objectives | To undertake a programme of education in the community | To provide well-planned access | | |

| Tactical objectives | To organise regular activities such as pond-dipping | To organise nature study sessions on site for local schools | To construct informal path alongside stream in attractive woodland | To construct steps down steep bank regularly used for access | To put up new fence in south corner to restrict access to path and discourage rubbish dumping |

Figure 5.1   Some of the objectives for a neglected site in Sheffield

general and long lasting, for example 'to improve wildlife diversity', 'to provide educational facilities'. At the intermediate level are management objectives, or policies, which are more immediate and less general, for example 'to encourage wildflowers in grassland'. At the bottom level are tactical objectives, or prescriptions, specifying precisely how the management objectives will be put into practice, for example 'the grass to be mown once a year in September and the cuttings removed'. An example of this way of sorting objectives is shown in Figure 5.1 for a neglected site in Sheffield.

There will always be a number of constraints on the type of management that can be undertaken; for example, resources may be limited, people may not have the time or the required skills, or the tenancy of the site may be insecure so that only short-term and inexpensive options with an immediate impact are worthwhile. Constraints need not necessarily be a permanent barrier to a particular course of action. It may be possible to find a way round them, if not immediately at least in the long term. Resources may eventually become available, people may be interested in attending training courses to acquire the necessary skills, site development may be postponed and the tenancy extended. It is therefore worth including in your plan options that you would like to adopt, but that appear out of the question at present, together with a note of the relevant constraints.

Working to a plan

A management plan can be devised by considering each habitat parcel in turn, exploring as many options for that habitat type as possible, and selecting the most appropriate options in the light of your objectives and constraints. If large enough, habitat parcels can be subdivided, or zoned, to allow a number of different objectives to be met.

Once options have been chosen and detailed prescriptions agreed, they should be recorded on a work plan. The plan should be simple to understand, and kept where it can be consulted easily by those involved in supervising or carrying out the work. Project proposals can be summarised in a simple annotated sketch map, based on the the map on the survey form,

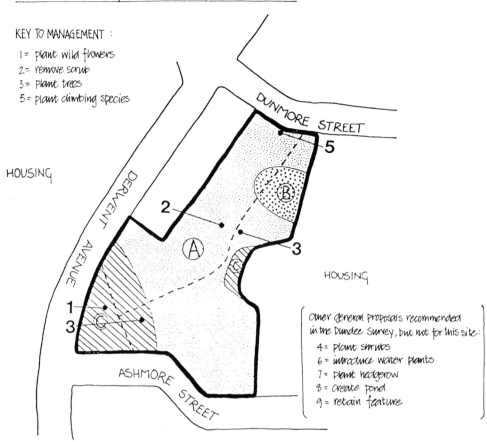

SITE: DISUSED QUARRY, DERWENT AVENUE

KEY TO MANAGEMENT:
1 = plant wild flowers
2 = remove scrub
3 = plant trees
5 = plant climbing species

HOUSING

DUNMORE STREET

DERWENT AVENUE

HOUSING

ASHMORE STREET

Other general proposals recommended
in the Dundee Survey, but not for this site:
4 = plant shrubs
6 = introduce water plants
7 = plant hedgerow
8 = create pond
9 = retain feature

Figure 5.2 Management proposals for a site in Dundee

as illustrated for one of the sites in the Dundee survey in Figure 5.2. For each project, the plan should include notes summarising:

▶ the objectives;
▶ the time of year when the task is to be done;
▶ the method to be used;
▶ the materials and equipment required;
▶ the costs involved and sources of funds;
▶ any legal or other constraints;
▶ safety precautions to be taken;
▶ any training needed;
▶ who is to do the work.

The work plan should include a suggested schedule, and show the order of priority among different projects.

Safety, training and legal requirements

Some tasks are intrinsically hazardous, especially when unskilled or young volunteers are involved, for example working with sharp tools, or near or in water. Except for the simplest tasks, people should not work alone. Insurance cover for volunteers is vital, and there must always be a first-aid box on site. Protective clothing should be worn if necessary, and helpers should be well briefed about how to avoid potential hazards. For some tasks, such as using a chain saw, training is essential. Training for a variety of conservation tasks is provided by organisations such as the British Trust for Conservation Volunteers and the Scottish Conservation Projects, as well as by the Agricultural Training Board. Legal requirements should be checked, for example those covering pesticide use and tree felling (see the *Legislation and Regulations* booklet with the foundation book).

Monitoring progress

It is important to keep accurate records of the date when each task was carried out, and of the source and type of any new species introduced to the site (such as wildflowers, or frog spawn), as an aid to long-term management planning. If appropriate, the information should be recorded on the site map. Photographs or slides taken at regular intervals from the same viewpoint (and, if possible, using the same camera and lens) provide a valuable visual record of progress, and can be used to inform visitors about the development of a site. Periodic reassessment of a site's wildlife value is needed to record species gained or lost and to show whether site conditions are changing. Management plans should be reviewed annually and revised every five years.

General conservation guidelines

For all habitat types, one of the first management decisions is likely to be how much management intervention is desirable or feasible. On sites or areas where conditions are changing extremely slowly, for example in naturally regenerating old woodland or on industrial waste sites that are gradually acquiring an interesting flora, a valid management option might be minimal intervention, allowing natural processes to proceed unchecked. Minimal intervention might also be considered for at least part of a site that is to be used mainly for educational purposes, since it would allow ecological processes such as colonisation and succession to be studied. However, on most urban sites, some form of management is needed.

There are some conservation guidelines that apply to most sites and habitat types. In general, appropriate management options will be those that meet the following aims:

▶ maintain or increase structural and species diversity;

▶ cause the minimum of disturbance to wildlife, either by ensuring operations occur in periods of dormancy or by working on small sections in rotation over a period of several years;

▶ maintain or introduce gradual transition zones between different types of habitat, since these areas are particularly valuable for wildlife;

▶ improve access for visitors, while protecting sensitive areas from disturbance, for example by careful siting of paths;

▶ keep sites litter-free.

5.2   Grassland habitats

Grassland forms by far the largest area of potential wildlife habitat in most towns and cities, generally occupying about one-third of the area. Of this, about two-thirds is closely mown amenity grassland and the rest is unmanaged.

The main options for grassland management involve:
- ▶ altering the mowing regime;
- ▶ introducing wildflowers;
- ▶ controlling unwanted species.

Mowing regime

Grass growth can be manipulated by mowing, grazing or burning, and by the use of fertilisers, herbicides and growth retardants. In most built-up areas, mowing is usually the most practical and cost-effective way of controlling growth on wildlife areas, although in some places grazing may be possible. The frequency, timing and height of mowing have an important influence on the species present in the grass, and can be used to alter species composition.

Fine grasses and flowers

In managed grassland, a more diverse and flower-rich sward can be encouraged by reducing the frequency of mowing. This option needs to be closely linked to your assessment of the characteristics of the grassland. It is only likely to be appropriate for sites that are infertile, as indicated by the presence of fine grasses such as fescues and bents. It may be worth experimenting with reduced mowing on trial areas for a year or more first, to establish which species are already present. **Scarifying** the grass with a rake or harrow can give seeds that remain in the soil seed bank a chance to germinate.

On promising sites, summer flowers can be encouraged by checking grass growth in May and again in September (cutting it to a height of 2–7 centimetres), but allowing free growth over the summer. In very dry conditions or where the growing season is short, only one cut may be necessary. Spring flowers can be encouraged by leaving the grass uncut until July to allow the flowers to set seed. The grass can then be cut regularly, or left uncut until September.

Long cut grass should be removed if possible to avoid smothering small plants. Ideally the cuttings should be left where they fall for a day or two before removal to allow any invertebrates they may be sheltering the opportunity to move away. Some local authorities, such as Leicester, have invested in machinery that allows the cut grass to be used as hay.

Wildflower lawns

In semi-formal areas, regular mowing can be discontinued briefly to allow particular species to flower, creating a wildflower lawn. For example, a break in mowing in June allows buttercups and daisies to flower, and a break in July or August, catsear and hawkbits.

Rotational mowing

Rotational mowing, allowing a proportion of the grass to remain uncut all year round, can be used to provide overwintering refuges for invertebrates and small mammals.

Coarse grassland

On fertile soils and sites dominated by vigorous species such as rye-grass and meadow-grass, reduced mowing is only likely to encourage coarse grasses, nettles, thistles and docks. Although this provides good habitat for invertebrates and small mammals, and attracts a variety of birds, it may not be the desired effect. Options for this type of grassland include reducing soil fertility and reseeding, as described in Chapter 6, or allowing succession to scrub, or planting up with trees.

General points

Continuity of management is important; if an area is mown for spring flowers one year and summer flowers the next, the end result may be a decline in plant diversity. However, variation in mowing regime across a site, with some areas always regularly mown and others always mown less frequently, will add to the wildlife value by increasing structural diversity. Where different mowing regimes are used on one site, it is helpful to show each cut on a separate map. This is essential if contractors are used, as otherwise the risk of mistakes is high.

The ground should be checked for obstacles before mowing begins, particularly if the grass is long. Regular clearance of litter and more frequent mowing around the edge of a site, and alongside footpaths and roads, helps create an impression of a well cared for site. Informal mown paths can be used to guide visitor access through long grassland. Mown paths that are heavily used may need to be repositioned to one side from time to time to allow worn grass a chance to recover. Alternatively, bare soil alongside paths can be left to provide sites on which solitary bees and wasps can dig nest burrows.

Grazing

For grazing to be feasible, sites need to be securely fenced, or the animals tethered and protected from harrassment and theft. Water must be available, and potential hazards to animals and people must be carefully considered. Animals that are quite used to people, such as pets and those from school or city farms, are likely to adjust most readily to sites with free access to the public. Rabbits, geese, goats, sheep, cattle and ponies can all be used, given appropriate conditions.

Grazing produces a less uniform sward than mowing. This can be an advantage for conservation since it creates a mosaic of different micro-environments (including the very interesting, if transient, one of dung).

Tall herb communities

Tall herb communities and unmanaged grassland can be mown once a year in the autumn where the dry dead stems and flowerheads are considered unsightly or a fire hazard, and to prevent succession to scrub, although this tidying up operation removes valuable overwinter shelter. For all flower-rich areas, the production of a chart, such as that in Figure 5.3(a), showing the main flowering periods of all the common species present can be a useful guide to decisions about the best time to mow. A more elaborate chart such as that shown in Figure 5.3(b) can be used to provide additional management information such as the height of the plants, the time when attractive foliage or berries are present, and how long less sightly dead vegetation is likely to remain obvious.

Introducing wildflowers

The number and type of flowers present in grassland can be increased by planting out pot-grown plants, transplanting turves from flower-rich areas or oversowing with wildflower seed. As with reduced mowing, successful results are most likely on infertile soils. If the site already has a high ecological value, seek expert advice before introducing new species.

The seeds or plants should be appropriate for the soil and climatic conditions of the site, preferably of locally typical wild varieties and, if possible, from local seed sources. Many seed merchants now supply wildflower seeds and seed mixes, but you should check the source since they sometimes include agricultural cultivars and seed from other countries.

For small areas, you may prefer to collect your own seed. Some rare plants are protected by law and their seed should not be collected without

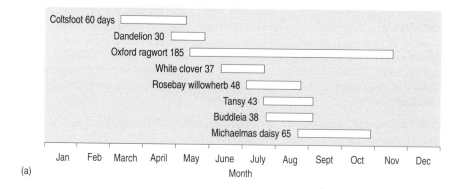

(a)

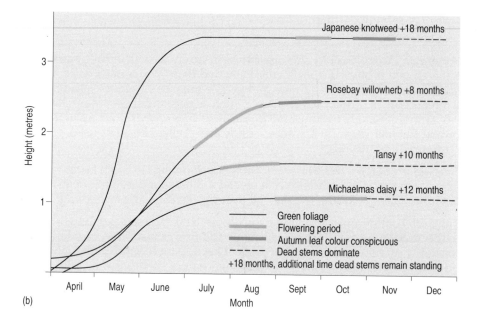

Figure 5.3 Chart showing (a) main flowering periods of dominant species on an urban wasteland site in Sheffield; (b) main visual characteristics of some common urban species and their periods of visibility (Source: Gilbert, 1989)

authorisation (see the *Legislation and Regulations* booklet with the foundation book). Even for common plants, only a small proportion of the seed should be removed. Ripe seed, once collected, should be dried slowly in a warm, well-ventilated area for two to four weeks, before storage in air-tight containers such as screw-top jars. Different types of seed should be stored separately and labelled with the plant name, and the place and date of collection.

Pot-grown plants

Seed can be germinated in pots and the plants transferred to gaps in the turf once they are established. This method, although time-consuming, has a good success rate. If necessary, gaps can be created by raking the ground or spot-spraying the grass with a systemic herbicide. Some seeds have specialised requirements for germination (for example many legumes have a hard seed coat and their germination is enhanced by scarifying, or scratching, the seed surface); common examples are listed in Table 5.1.

Transplanting turves

Occasionally, when flower-rich grassland elsewhere has to be developed as building land, it may be possible to rescue turves and transplant them (provided that conditions are similar) as a way of enriching the wildlife on your site. This method has the advantage of also transferring invertebrate species.

74

Table 5.1 Species whose seeds may require special treatment before sowing

Germination enhanced by scarification prior to sowing

Black medick	Cranesbills, storksbills	Salad burnet
Broom	Horseshoe vetch	Trefoils
Clovers	Kidney vetch	Vetches
Common rockrose	Melilots	Vetchlings, everlasting peas
Common storksbill	Sainfoin	

Germination enhanced by cold treatment (6 weeks at 0–4oC) or by sowing in autumn

Burnet saxifrage	Dyer's rocket, weld	Wild carrot
Clustered bellflower	Great burnet	

Germination enhanced by moist storage at 5oC *

Alexanders (11)	Gipsy-wort (9)	Purging flax (2)
Alpine lady's mantle (19)	Globe flower (8)	Red rattle (3)
Burnet saxifrage (2)	Goosegrass (1)	Scarlet pimpernel (13)
Carnation-grass (18)	Greater burnet saxifrage (11)	Shepherd's purse (10)
Common agrimony (3)	Greater celandine (3)	Small balsam (4)
Common butterwort (2)	Ground elder (12)	Small toadflax (1)
Common sedge (1)	Hairy violet (14)	Smooth sedge (5)
Common spike-rush (19)	Hedge woundwort (8)	Soapwort (2)
Common violet (3)	Honeysuckle (4)	Sweet cicely (1)
Corn mint (18)	Large campanula (1)	Unbranched bur-reed (1)
Cow parsley (3)	Long-headed poppy (2)	Upright hedge parsley (8)
Cowslip (6)	Marsh marigold (3)	Vervain (3)
Cuckoo-pint (6)	Marsh violet (3)	Water mint (1)
Field angelica (3)	Mountain pansy (5)	Woody nightshade (6)
Field pansy (3)	Pepper saxifrage (10)	Yellow archangel (6)
Field poppy (3)	Pignut (9)	Yellow rattle (3)

*Numbers in parentheses indicate duration of treatment in months.
(Source: Emery, 1986, quoted from Wells *et al.*, 1981 and Grimes *et al.*, 1981)

Oversowing wildflower mixes

Grassland can be oversown with a wildflower seed mix in September, after first scarifying the ground with a rake, a spiked harrow or a rotovator. Alternatively, a slot seeder can be used. This opens up a strip in the turf, into which the seed is planted. Oversowing is less reliable than the other two methods.

Controlling unwanted species

Unwanted weeds can be controlled by cutting them before they flower and set seed, or by hand-pulling, or by careful spot-treatment with recommended herbicides, depending on the species. In Germany, an infra-red gun is used for weed control. All plants have some value for wildlife, so that removal is only necessary if they are causing a problem; for example, if unchecked growth threatens to displace more desirable species, if they are likely to poison stock, or if they are considered socially unacceptable because they signify neglect and decay.

Plants that readily regrow from stout roots, such as broad-leaved dock and horse radish, or that can spread by vegetative means, such as creeping thistle and Japanese knotweed, may need repeated herbicide treatment if regrowth appears.

5.3   Woodland habitats

The main conservation management options for woodland involve:

▶ thinning;

▶ **coppicing**;

▶ opening up glades and rides;

▶ underplanting with trees, shrubs and flowers.

Other measures that improve the wildlife interest and amenity value of woods include retaining dead wood, installing nest boxes, and clearing litter.

The selection of management options for woodland is made easier if the woodland is divided into distinctive zones or compartments. Your wildlife assessment should allow you to identify zones on the basis of the dominant tree species, tree age, soil type or particular features such as glades or paths. These compartments can then be considered separately in deciding on appropriate management options.

If your group has neither the experience nor the resources to tackle the management of the woodland as a whole, you can still enhance the wildlife value by concentrating your activities on the woodland edge, rides, glades and other such features. These transitional habitats are particularly valuable for wildlife and are the areas most visible to the public. In any case, beware of overmanagement, which may be unnecessary and can do more harm than good.

Thinning

Thinning may be necessary to allow light in and encourage regeneration and **understorey** development, to check the spread of unwanted species, and to make safe damaged or dead wood. To minimise disturbance to wildlife, thinning should be restricted to the winter months from October to early March. In general, felling is best left to experienced contractors, although small areas or individual trees may be tackled by group members provided they have received adequate training and follow all the recommended safety procedures. The trees to be removed should be clearly marked, for example with tape or paint.

Coppicing

Coppicing is the traditional form of management in many old woods, especially those that consist mainly of hazel, hornbeam, sweet chestnut and, in some parts of the country, small-leaved lime. Other trees that can be coppiced include alder, ash, beech, birch, elm, field maple, sessile oak and willow.

Coppicing was used to provide a regular supply of timber poles for building, hedge laying and fencing, and firewood. It involves cutting the tree trunk near ground level, which encourages several new stems to develop from the cut base, or stool. In some coppiced woodland, the best trees are kept and grown on to provide timber; this form of management is known as 'coppice with standards'.

Coppicing can have considerable benefits for conservation. Since small sections (**coupes**) of woodland are usually coppiced in rotation, the result is a diverse woodland structure that encourages a diversity of wildlife. The increase in light after cutting stimulates the growth of the ground flora, which is usually at its best in the second or third year of the rotation. Conditions are generally best for birds between the sixth and eighth year, or before shade reduces the understorey cover. Each rotation may be up to 30 years, although a 7–15 year rotation is recommended for wildlife.

If you are thinking of introducing or reintroducing coppicing, it may be best to experiment initially with a small trial area. If the site was originally waste land or is on fertile soil, or if conditions have changed since the wood was last coppiced, invasive species such as bramble may take over when light is allowed in.

Overcrowded coppice can be thinned to promote the growth of a single stem from each stool, resulting in a change to **high forest** management. Gappy coppice can be improved by planting saplings in the gaps at the time the trees are coppiced, or by pegging down stems to touch the ground and covering them with soil to encourage rooting (a practice termed **layering**, illustrated in Figure 5.4).

In old pasture woodland, where stock once grazed under widely spaced trees, **pollarding** is the traditional form of management. Pollarding involves cutting back the main trunk of the tree to a height of about 2 metres instead of near ground level, so protecting the regrowth from grazing.

Opening up glades and rides

Glades, rides and the woodland edge can provide a sunny, sheltered and humid environment, which is good for a variety of wildlife, particularly butterflies and birds. The aim should be to provide a graded edge, where ground flora, herb layer, understorey and **canopy** are all present, as shown in Figure 5.5 (overleaf). This may involve thinning some trees at the edge to let in more light and, if necessary, underplanting with small trees, shrubs and woodland flowers.

Figure 5.4   Layering to fill a gap

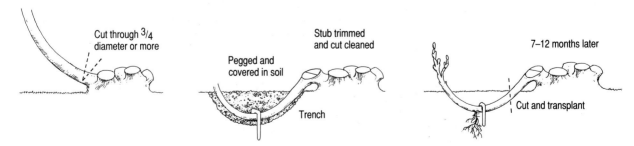

77

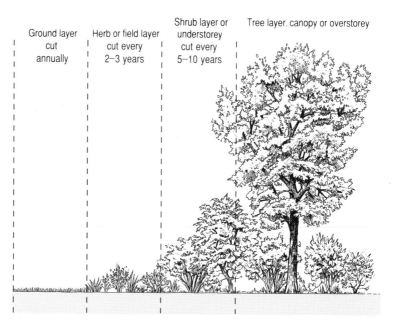

Ground layer
cut
annually

Herb or field layer
cut every
2–3 years

Shrub layer or
understorey
cut every
5–10 years

Tree layer, canopy or overstorey

Figure 5.5 Management of woodland edge to provide a graded structure

The graded edge can be maintained by cutting back vigorously growing shrubs every 5 to 10 years on a rotational basis to prevent smaller plants being smothered. The herb layer can be cut every 2 or 3 years, preferably by cutting only short sections annually, to ensure there is always some overwintering and feeding habitat left, especially for invertebrates like butterflies. Grassy paths can be mown more regularly, as necessary to allow access.

Rides will be more sheltered if they are not set out in straight lines but curve or alter direction. Glades are more valuable if they are linked by rides, so providing a greater area of continuous habitat of a similar type. Other areas within woodland that provide valuable habitat and should be retained include rocky outcrops, streams, ponds and marshy ground.

Underplanting with trees, shrubs and flowers

Gaps, rides and the woodland edge can be planted with locally common wild species of small trees and shrubs. Shade-tolerant species include hazel, holly and bird cherry. Any weed growth should be kept down around the young plants until they are well established.

Underplanting improves the variation in woodland structure, provides warmth and cover for wildlife and adds visual interest. Underplanting can also be used amongst scattered groups of parkland trees to develop small patches of woodland. Planting of woodland flowers, such as bluebell, wood anemone and wild periwinkle, adds extra interest.

Other measures

Dead wood and over-mature trees are essential as habitat for many fungi, invertebrates and hole-nesting birds, so should be retained provided they do not pose a public hazard. Birds and bats can be encouraged by attaching artificial nest and bat boxes to mature trees.

Litter should be cleared from paths regularly but, in less accessible areas of wood, litter clearance should be restricted to winter months to minimise the disturbance to birds.

Scrub management

Scrub forms a transitional stage in the succession from tall herbs and grassland to woodland. Apart from keeping it down to maintain or restore grassland habitat, or allowing it to progress to woodland, one management option is to try and retain and enhance it since it provides good cover for small mammals and birds.

A varied structure can be achieved by selective cutting and clearing to prevent the scrub forming inpenetrable thickets that exclude the light. Clearing should be undertaken early in the year, before March, to avoid disturbance to nesting birds and to allow any fruits to be eaten. As in the case of other drastic management changes, only a proportion should be cut back in any one year, with the aim of achieving a mosaic of different age classes.

Scrub can be cut every 5 or 6 years to prevent small bushes and young trees closing over, or at longer intervals (approximately 15–20 years) to prevent succession to woodland. Cutting encourages the development of multiple stems so that the regrowth is likely to be dense. For some species, regrowth can be weakened by cutting the scrub close enough to the ground to allow regular mowing for 4 or 5 years. For others, careful herbicide treatment may be necessary to limit regrowth.

Hedge management

Hedges can be managed by regular trimming every two or three years. Unmanaged hedges and those that are gappy at the base can be restored by **laying** or coppicing. As in the case of scrub and woodland, it is best to deal with small sections in rotation and to confine management to the winter months, ideally between January and early March (except in frost, which may damage exposed tissue).

In general, the greater the volume of a hedge the better it is for wildlife, especially nesting birds. Trees in a hedge provide songposts and additional nesting sites. Hedges can be trimmed to a variety of shapes, but a triangular profile, or A-shape, is usually recommended for wildlife purposes because it provides a gradation in the structure of the hedge, so increasing habitat diversity. If mechanical cutting is used, the implement should be appropriate for the size of wood to be trimmed. Thick woody stems should be trimmed with a shape saw rather than by flailing, which leaves unsightly jagged stems. Sturdy saplings within a hedge can be tagged with a tape or plastic marker so that they can be avoided during trimming and allowed to develop into hedgerow trees.

A hedge that is to be laid needs to be about 2.5–5 metres tall. Selected stems are partially severed close to the ground, lowered sideways along the line of the hedge and held in place as shown in Figure 5.6 (overleaf). Laying is a skilled task but can be undertaken by volunteers after training. It promotes the development of healthy young shoots from the base of the hedge and along the cut stem, producing an attractive and dense barrier.

Like laying, coppicing can be used to restore a neglected hedge, although the regrowth is not so vigorous, a small proportion of coppiced stools may die and the resulting hedge is not stockproof for at least the first two years. Its advantages are that it requires less skill and is less time-consuming than hedge laying.

Figure 5.6   Completing a laid hedge

Very old neglected hedges, or those that contain a variety of different shrubs and trees, may need to be managed by a combination of trimming, laying and coppicing according to the condition and type of woody plants present.

The perennial vegetation at the base of the hedge, and any adjacent verge, bank or ditch, contribute significantly to a hedge's habitat value and should be retained. The ground vegetation should not be removed since it could allow colonisation by invasive annual species such as cleavers.

5.4   Aquatic habitats

The main management options for aquatic habitats involve:

▶   clearing silt and debris;

▶   managing the vegetation;

▶   monitoring the water level and pollution.

Clearing silt and debris

Areas of still and slow-flowing water, especially small areas such as ponds and ditches, can rapidly silt up and change from an aquatic environment to a terrestrial one. Periodic dredging may therefore be necessary. The openings of any culverts and land drains that feed into the water need regular checking to ensure that they remain unblocked.

Dredging is very disruptive for aquatic wildlife. It is best done in winter, between October and March. Even then, some species will inevitably be disturbed, so that only small sections (for example, alternate sides of a ditch or one-third of a pond) should be dredged in any one year. This leaves some vegetation and undisturbed mud as a refuge from which recolonisation can occur. Overwintering wildfowl rely on inland water between December and February, so where a site is important for these birds dredging should be completed earlier.

Silt can be removed by hand with a shovel, or by using a mechanical digger or suction dredger. Mechanical dredging cannot be used on artificially lined ponds, and should be used with great care on areas that are clay-lined. Where heavy machinery is to be used, work should be done when the adjacent land is dry or frozen to minimise soil compaction. Alternatively, mats or rafts can be laid on the ground to help spread the load.

80

The excavated sediment is nutrient-rich and may contain heavy metals and other pollutants, so it is best removed from the site. Clumps of plants removed during excavation can be kept to one side in waterlogged conditions and replanted once the work is complete, or used to stock other less well vegetated ponds and ditches nearby.

Dredging provides an opportunity to improve the value of aquatic habitats by altering the profile of the base and banks, providing they are not artificially lined. The depth of ponds and ditches can be varied by excavating deeper holes or channels in places; areas where the water depth is greater than 1.5–2 metres can provide valuable refuges for aquatic animals when shallower water is frozen in winter. The creation of sections of gently shelving bank provides conditions suitable for a variety of plant types and access points for birds and small animals. Excavation of a shallow underwater **berm**, or ledge, along one side of a ditch provides good habitat for many invertebrates. In artificially lined ponds and lakes with vertical sides, stone-filled wire mesh baskets (**gabions**) can be positioned at the sides to provide shallow areas in which to root **emergent aquatic plants**, such as lesser spearwort (see Figure 5.7).

Altering the profile

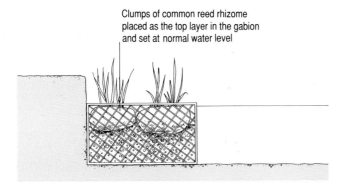

Clumps of common reed rhizome placed as the top layer in the gabion and set at normal water level

Figure 5.7   Use of gabion to provide a shallow area for emergent vegetation

Anyone working in or near deep or flowing water should be able to swim, and there should always be someone watching from the bank. Waders or boots with a good grip should be worn as surfaces are likely to be slippery. The depth of the water should be tested with a stick before stepping into the next section. Deep areas should be marked with clearly visible poles.

Safety

Managing the vegetation

Emergent vegetation at the water's edge may need controlling if it is encouraging damaging amounts of silt and debris to accumulate or if competitive species such as greater reedmace, reed sweet-grass or rushes are spreading and displacing more valued species. Growth can be controlled by cutting the plants back or digging them out. Common reed is best controlled by cutting it at the time of most vigorous growth, in July, but other species can be cut back during the winter to minimise disturbance. In the winter, cutting the plants above the water level allows frost to restrict growth, whereas at other times of year the vegetation should be cut below the water level to restrict growth by limiting the uptake of oxygen.

Aquatic vegetation

Occasionally, floating plants such as water lilies may need to be controlled if they cover the water and shade out submerged plants. Excessive growth of duckweeds and algae on the surface of the water indicates high nutrient levels. The growth can be removed with long-handled rakes or by dragging a floating boom across the water, but it is likely to persist unless the cause of the nutrient enrichment can be tracked down and checked. Late summer or autumn is the best time to remove the weed. Care is needed because some algal blooms are toxic to humans and other mammals.

Cut vegetation should be cleared from the water and left on the bankside temporarily (but not where it might smother valued plants) to allow attached aquatic animals to return to the water.

Plant diversity can be increased by introducing locally occurring species from nearby sites, as described in Chapter 6. Invasive species such as Canadian pondweed, Australian swamp stonecrop, water fern or sweet flag should be avoided.

Bankside vegetation

Shrubs and trees along the bankside provide valuable cover for wildlife and may be encouraged to protect a proportion of the bankside from disturbance by visitors. Some shading of the water by trees can be a useful way of controlling excessive aquatic vegetation. However, shrubby bankside vegetation and overhanging trees on the south side may need to be cut back to allow in light, and to provide some access along the water's edge. Trees such as willow and alder can be pollarded or coppiced to control their growth. Trees may need to be removed if there is a risk of their roots damaging artificial pond liners or water-retaining earthworks.

Reeds, sedge beds and wet grassland can be mown or grazed occasionally to remove old vegetation and prevent succession to scrub. Marshy areas can be mown when the ground is frozen.

Monitoring the water level and pollution

Water level

The water level of artificially lined ponds should be regularly monitored to ensure that the lining remains watertight. Small artificially lined ponds may need to be kept topped up in summer with fresh water from a standpipe or bowser (water tank).

Although fluctuations in water level harm some forms of wildlife, they can also be beneficial. Shallow areas and exposed mud in the autumn and winter can provide valuable feeding grounds for wading birds. Fluctuating water levels are important for specialised plants such as mudwort.

Pollution

Litter should be regularly removed by hand or by nets. Storm water run-off from roads and car parks can be diverted into freely draining holding lagoons or channels to prevent it running directly into ponds. Silt traps and oil interceptors can be installed but must be regularly cleaned if they are to remain effective.

If you notice serious or persistent pollution of a watercourse from external sources, for example from the release of untreated sewage or industrial waste, the only practical course of action may be to report the matter to the local authority's environmental health officer, the National Rivers Authority (in England and Wales) or the River Purification Board (in Scotland).

5.5 Exercise 5: Choosing management options for your site

Carry out this exercise for the site you have already assessed. If the existing ecological value of all or part of the site is limited, combine this exercise with that at the end of Chapter 6 before finally selecting options.

1   Check through the options described in this chapter for any that apply to your site. If possible, supplement the information given here with ideas obtained from other books, by visiting other similar sites and by consulting other urban conservation groups.

2   Select the options that you consider are most appropriate, in the light of the objectives and constraints you have identified during your assessment.

3   Summarise the options on a sketch map of the site, and draw up a brief work plan.

5.6   Case study example of managing a site

Crabtree Pond and Wood, Sheffield

In 1986, Sheffield City Wildlife Trust was approached for advice by local residents who were concerned about the state of Crabtree Pond and the woodland surrounding it.

The pond was created in the late nineteenth century as an ornamental feature in the grounds of a private house. Originally on the urban fringe, it is now part of the inner city and surrounded by high density housing. The pond passed into public ownership in the 1970s and was managed for coarse fishing for several years. High levels of vandalism coupled with a shortage of resources then forced the local authority to reduce its management. By the mid-1980s the site looked very neglected and had a bad reputation. Even so, it was identified as being of moderate to high wildlife value by the Trust's inner city habitat survey.

The Trust agreed to take on the management of the site, working in partnership with the local community. The main objectives were those already described in Figure 5.1. A comprehensive survey of the site was carried out by a group of landscape architecture students from Sheffield University, who divided the site into eight distinct zones, as shown in Figure 5.8 (overleaf). For each zone they defined the main problems and outlined possible management options, as described below.

Zone A is a vital part of the site because it provides some of the first views into the wood and to the pond. It includes sycamore, poplar and ornamental hawthorn scattered in mown grass. Despite the mowing, it suggests an underused and uncared-for open space. Shade is too heavy in places, so some areas are often bare and muddy in winter.

Zone A Main entrance area

Management proposals involve selective felling of the sycamore and poplar, combined with new planting of more attractive trees and shrubs with both amenity and wildlife value. This will open up the entrance area, providing attractive views into the site. Grass mowing should continue, to show that the area is being actively managed and to discourage rubbish dumping.

The steep slope down to the pond has been eroded by foot and bike traffic. Litter and rubbish have been tipped and trees vandalised. The dense tree canopy and soil erosion have prevented the establishment of shrub understorey and ground flora on the steeper banks.

Zone B Southern corner

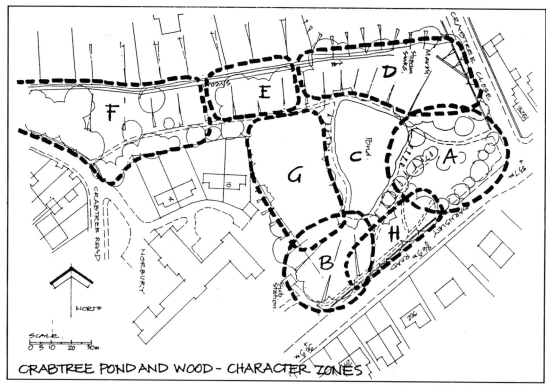

Figure 5.8   Crabtree Pond and Wood, showing distinctive character zones

The desire for access at this corner should be recognised by the construction of steps down the steep bank. Terracing and planting of the slope will arrest erosion and control access. Felling of sycamore will allow light in, encouraging plant growth and creating a more open and inviting entrance.

Zone C The pond

The pond is the main focus of the site. It has little marginal vegetation, partly because of the hard edges of concrete and timber and probably also because of fluctuating water levels. A steady flow from a leak on the north side has been observed in both summer and winter. As with many other areas of the site, the pond suffers from accumulations of litter.

Restoration work on the pond is likely to be costly and require expert help, but is important to the upgrading of the site. The existing concrete paths can be used as a base for more attractive paving and the remaining banks reshaped to provide shallow areas for the planting and establishment of marginal aquatic vegetation. The shallow slopes would reduce the risk to children.

Zone D Lower stream valley

The marshy area of woodland is kept wet by water leaking from the pond and a stream running along the northern edge of the site. Recent rises in the water table are indicated by several dead and dying trees. Heavy shade cast by a dense canopy of closely spaced sycamore trees has impoverished the ground flora so that there is little marsh vegetation. A stone retaining wall is in a bad state of repair.

Thinning of the dense tree cover is essential in this area to allow planting and the establishment of understorey trees and shrubs on the valley slope down to

84

the stream. Clearance of the standing dead and dying trees and repairs to the stone wall are needed to make this a more attractive and safer area.

Zone E is an attractive area of sycamore woodland consisting of more mature trees with a dense and moderately diverse herb layer. A surfaced path provides access.

Zone E Central section of stream valley

The only work required here in the short term is the construction of an informal path along the stream and connecting to the existing path. This will give better access to what is already an attractive part of the wood.

A wooded valley follows the stream between an area of housing and an old people's home. Some felling of sycamore and diseased elm here has created a more open woodland with large glades, supporting a richer and more attractive understorey than elsewhere on the site. A collapsed boundary fence along the stream has allowed the slope to be used as a short cut and a play area, resulting in soil erosion.

Zone F Upper stream valley

Some of the glades should be restocked to increase the diversity of tree species and ensure a healthy age distribution. The construction of steps is required where the footpath enters the site from Crabtree Road.

Zone G is a dense stand of mostly even-aged young trees. The high proportion of ash, which has a light canopy and is late coming into leaf, has allowed the development of luxurious ground vegetation.

Zone G Young ash and sycamore woodland

Thinning is required to allow lateral development of the better trees. Sycamore rather than ash should be removed, to encourage the development of ash-dominated woodland and its associated diverse understorey.

A strip of woodland, mainly sycamore and poplar, forms an important screen between the pond and the busy main road.

Zone H Barnsley Road boundary

Selective thinning is required, in combination with new planting with a good proportion of evergreen shrubs and trees, to maintain a dense screen as a buffer to the noise, atmospheric pollution and traffic.

Continuing management of the site should include: regular litter clearance; weed control around new planting; periodic clearance of excess aquatic vegetation; regular summer mowing of grass in the entrance zone; periodic inspection of trees for health and safety; maintenance of paths and fence and repairs to any vandalism damage; and further selective thinning in the woodland in 8 to 10 years' time.

Following lengthy negotiations, Sheffield City Council approved these proposals and supported the Trust's bid for Urban Programme funding. Local schools, local residents, Woodcraft Folk, Scouts and Guides, Youth Training Scheme and Employment Training trainees, Conservation Volunteers and members of Sheffield City Wildlife Trust have all been involved in putting the plan into practice. Large numbers of daffodil bulbs have been planted at the main entrance to the site to improve its appearance in the spring. The concrete paths around the pond have not been paved since this proposal was regarded as both expensive and impractical. An informal committee, comprising members of the Wildlife Trust and local residents, has been formed to arrange future work on the site. Clean-ups are held every month or so, plus activities such as pond-dipping to study the aquatic wildlife. The site is now regularly used for nature study by several local schools.

(Source: Roger Butterfield, Sheffield City Wildlife Trust, and University of Sheffield students)

Chapter 6

CREATING NEW HABITATS

Urban development and redevelopment may threaten existing habitats but also provide challenging new opportunities for habitat creation. While newly created habitats cannot replicate rich plant and animal communities such as ancient woodland and old pasture that have taken centuries to develop, they can rapidly acquire a natural appearance with far greater value for wildlife than formally landscaped areas. The greater choice of management options and design input that are possible on a new site can allow a wide range of objectives to be met.

Wherever possible, existing habitats should be retained and incorporated into the design and landscaping of new developments. Habitat creation should be restricted to areas that have little or no existing wildlife value, such as underused areas of species-poor amenity grassland, disturbed land around new housing and commercial developments, and hard surfaced areas such as playgrounds.

The aim for habitat creation should be to incorporate any existing vegetation, work with existing site conditions and use locally common wild plants, rather than to create a totally artificial landscape involving major earthworks, imported soil and cultivated species. Habitats established by working with existing conditions and making the most of natural colonisation and succession are likely to be less costly to create and maintain, more in keeping with the character of the surroundings, and more attractive to wildlife. They also allow the development of local individuality rather than 'off-the-peg' uniformity.

This chapter discusses general aspects of site design and access, before describing some of the options available for creating three major habitat types: grassland, woodland, and aquatic habitats. It concludes with an exercise in site design for you to carry out, together with a case study example.

6.1   Site design

As with the management of existing habitats, the plan should be based on an assessment of the existing character of the site and its surroundings. The characteristics of any adjoining areas of vegetation, such as railway cuttings and gardens, should be noted since these may serve as sources of colonisation for the site and can indicate the type of plants that are likely to grow well.

Variations in conditions across the site need to be identified and taken into account in the design. Waterlogged or compacted soil, sloping ground, shaded areas and patches of rubble can all add interest to the layout, as can any existing geological, archaeological or architectural features. Previous uses of the site may have an important influence on site design, for example if building foundations remain. The position of underground services, such as sewers, may be a constraint.

Landscaping and planting can be used to emphasise the most attractive or important features on the site, or visible from it, and to disguise or soften unsightly features. On level featureless sites, some earthmoving may be needed to add interest by excavating ponds or hollows, and using the excavated soil to create slopes and mounds. Where these mounds are of reasonable size and include rubble they can act as islands on which the more interesting species of invertebrates from the earlier stages of colonisation can survive. If soil needs to be brought on to the site, it should be infertile subsoil or brick rubble rather than topsoil, to check the growth of the more invasive species and encourage plant diversity.

Objectives and constraints can be used to guide the type and range of habitats to include on the site. Within the limits imposed by the size of the site, the more different habitats that can be accommodated, the more useful the site will be as an educational resource. The design should allow space for transitional zones between different habitat types, because of both their value for wildlife and their implications for management. Habitats with abrupt boundaries between them are likely to require more intensive management to maintain their distinctive character than those where the boundaries are diffuse.

Above all, the design of the site should take into account the character and needs of the local community if the site is to be appreciated and cared for. Local people must be consulted, their needs identified and their ideas taken into account. This may involve establishing different zones for particular purposes, for example for a children's playground, a picnic area or a dog walking area, provided they are not intrusive and fit in with the site as a whole.

6.2   Access and path layout

The layout of paths can be of key significance in site design. The appropriate balance between encouraging public recreation and protecting wildlife from disturbance is likely to vary considerably between sites, but careful design of paths can ensure both objectives are met even on heavily used sites.

Paths need to be designed to take visitors past as many features of interest on the site as possible, while at the same time avoiding sensitive or hazardous areas. Paths that all loop back to the entrance are helpful for visitors who are unfamiliar with the site, especially if no signposting is used.

Curved paths are more interesting for visitors than a regular grid of tracks, although people may deviate from the track and take short-cuts if the route is unnecessarily tortuous. If costly permanent paths are planned, it is a good idea to begin with temporary tracks and base the permanent layout on those that are most frequently used.

The site design can incorporate 'buffer' zones, near the site entrance, around car parks and along the main paths, with picnic tables and mown grass, for visitors who are mainly interested in recreation.

To protect more sensitive wildlife areas from disturbance, it may be possible to provide viewpoints overlooking the area rather than allowing access through it. Alternatively, it may be possible to section the area so that only a proportion is accessible at any one time. To avoid unintentional damage to wildflower meadows, temporary tracks can be created by mowing to encourage vistors to keep to a clearly defined track. Raised walkways can be constructed across wet areas to avoid damage to marsh plants, although features of this sort must be well maintained to prevent accidents and the possibility of a claim for damages.

Where it is necessary to restrict access, natural barriers are preferable to fences and 'Keep Out' signs. Piles of cut branches and dead wood soon form an inpenetrable barrier if brambles are allowed to grow up through them, as well as providing additional habitat. Alternatively, a thorny hedge or a thicket of attractive berry-bearing shrubs can be used. A ground cover of shrubs with a prostrate growth habit, such as some types of pyracantha, or a wide ditch can be equally effective as a barrier without obscuring the view.

6.3   Creating grassland habitat

Preparing the site

Sites where it is intended to create grassland habitat should not be too thoroughly prepared, since fertile, well-cultivated and well-drained soils tend to encourage the more vigorously growing species to become dominant. Sites where the conditions are stressed in some way, for example those which are very dry, waterlogged or low in nitrogen, are most likely to develop a diverse flora, as mentioned in Chapter 5.

Fertile sites may be better planted with trees since trees thrive on rich soil and will soon outgrow competitors. Alternatively, a layer of topsoil can be removed (about 10 centimetres deep) and replaced with nutrient-poor material such as crushed concrete, which can be rotovated in before sowing begins.

Imported materials can also be used to vary conditions across the site. For example, clay can be used to create areas of impeded drainage; alkaline industrial waste can be used to counter acid conditions or encourage a calcareous flora to develop.

On flat sites, soil can be excavated from some areas and mounded up in others to create a more varied topography. Land drains can be blocked up to create marshy areas. Alternatively, it may be possible to divert some water from a nearby watercourse, but in this case the National Rivers Authority (in England and Wales) must first be consulted.

If an inpenetrable hard pan has formed near the soil surface as a result of soil compaction or the presence of consolidated industrial waste, this can either be roughly broken up, or left as it is to provide stressed conditions. Before seed is sown, a fine firm seedbed should be prepared, although cultivation does not need to be very deep. Once cultivated, the ground should be allowed time to settle before sowing. At sowing, any weeds should be cleared, and the soil surface lightly raked and rolled.

Selecting and sowing seed

As mentioned in Chapter 5, the choice of grasses and wildflowers to use should be guided by site conditions, in particular the pH, soil moisture levels, soil fertility, and extent of shade or light. Selection of the main grass species may need to be governed by the amount of visitor traffic expected.

Wildflower and grass seed can be purchased either as individual species or in mixtures that are appropriate for particular conditions. An example of a wildflower seed catalogue entry is shown in Table 6.1. If purchased seed is used, its origin should be checked, as mentioned in Chapter 5. Some seed mixtures include a **nurse crop**, such as Westerwolds rye-grass. This forms an

Table 6.1 Example of a wildflower/grass seed catalogue mixture for general short ground cover (figures are percentage by weight)

This mixture contains a large number of species for use on a wide range of soil types. Excessively acidic or alkaline soils are not recommended.

Wildflowers	
Birdsfoot trefoil	1.5
Bladder campion	0.5
Bulbous buttercup	0.5
Clustered bellflower	0.75
Cowslip	1.0
Hoary plantain	0.5
Lady's bedstraw	0.5
Meadowsweet	0.5
Meadow buttercup	1.5
Meadow saxifrage	0.25
Musk mallow	0.5
Ox-eye daisy	1.5
Ragged robin	2.0
Ribwort plantain	1.5
Rough hawkbit	0.5
Self-heal	2.0
Small scabious	0.5
Sorrel	0.5
White campion	2.0
Wild carrot	1.0
Yarrow	0.5
	20.0

Grasses	
Chewings fescue	20.0
Common bent grass	4.0
Crested dogstail	5.0
Dwarf creeping fescue	30.0
Quaking grass	1.0
Smooth-stalked meadow grass	20.0
	80.0

(Source: Phytomer Seeds, 1990)

open sward that provides shelter for more delicate species without crowding them out. The nurse crop usually needs to be cut back before it sets seed to prevent it taking over in succeeding years, although in some cases, particularly on infertile soils, it may die out naturally.

For sowing small areas, it may be possible to use locally collected seed, as mentioned in Chapter 5, or to purchase grass seed but mix it with the seed of local wildflowers. If necessary, locally collected seed can be multiplied by establishing a wildflower nursery, although this may take two years before any quantity of seed is produced. Fresh hay bales, grass clippings, or even soil, from flower-rich meadows can be spread over the site to serve as a source of seed. If this method is used, hay and clippings should be removed once seed has been shed, to avoid smothering the germinating seedlings.

Seed mixtures may separate out during storage and so should be remixed before sowing. Adding an equal amount of sand or sawdust to the seed helps ensure a more even distribution. The seed should be incorporated into the soil surface by raking or harrowing, and be lightly trampled or rolled to improve contact with the soil.

Until a sward is established, the seedbed may need to be watered to prevent it drying out. Vigorously growing weeds may need to be checked by hand-pulling, spot-treatment with a systemic herbicide, or with an infra-red gun. If the sward can be mown every two months to a height of about 8 to 10 centimetres during the first year, and the clippings removed, this will control the more competitive species and encourage the development of a diverse flora.

Wildflowers can be introduced into an existing grass sward by transplanting pot-grown plants or turves rather than sowing seed, as described in Chapter 5.

6.4   Creating woodland and scrub

Areas of scrub and woodland add structure and landscape interest to a new site, as well as providing valuable habitat. Although newly planted scrub and closely planted trees for coppicing can form dense cover within five or six years, woodland with standard trees takes at least 20 years to begin to mature, so that the expected length of tenancy of the site and likely availability of resources for maintenance in the long term need to be considered at the planning stage.

Selecting species

It is important to select species that are appropriate for the site conditions and to choose mixtures that will grow well together, ideally based on naturally occurring associations of woodland plants. Any self-set trees already on the site, and those that grow well nearby, provide a good guide to the types that are likely to thrive. Indeed, it is worth searching for any tree seedlings that are already present and nurturing *them*, rather than planting out bought-in seedlings. Some of the trees and shrubs that are most suited to urban conditions are listed in Table 6.2.

Some species may cause problems in particular situations, especially near buildings and alongside roads. Oak, lime, beech, hornbeam and ash, for example, grow to a considerable size and may block out light, obscure the view, interfere with overhead wires and cables or obstruct tall vehicles. Their roots may undermine walls and buildings. Lopping is expensive and can be unsightly, so that smaller or more upright trees may be needed for these situations. Poplar and willow should not be planted too close to buildings or land drains, since they have a high water uptake and shallow spreading roots that can block underground pipes, dry out clay soils and cause buildings to crack.

Planning the planting

Planting trees and shrubs is more costly than sowing grassland, and unsatisfactory results are more obvious and less easy to change, so that careful

Table 6.2 Woodland plants suitable for urban conditions

	Site conditions*												
	1	2	3	4	5	6	7	8	9	10	11	12	13
Trees													
Alder		●	●			●	●						●
Ash	●							●	●				
Beech		●						●					
Birch: hairy		●						●	●				
Birch: silver				●			●	●	●	●	●	●	
Blackthorn	●	●		●			●	●					
Broom									●	●	●		
Cherry: bird	●												
Cherry: gean	●												
Crab apple	●												
Hornbeam	●								●				
Lime: large-leaved	●					●							
Lime: small-leaved	●												
Maple: field	●						●						
Mountain ash	●						●				●		
Oak: pedunculate	●	●	●	●									
Oak: sessile	●					●							
Poplar: white		●					●						
Whitebeam: common							●	●	●				
Woodland edge/scrub													
Dogwood	●						●						
Elder		●		●		●	●	●	●		●	●	
Hawthorn: Midland	●	●		●			●	●	●		●		
Hawthorn: common	●	●					●	●	●				
Hazel	●						●	●					
Holly	●						●	●	●				
Honeysuckle	●	●		●			●						
Ivy	●			●		●	●	●	●				
Osier: common	●	●	●				●						
Privet: wild	●						●						
Rose: burnet	●						●	●	●		●		
Rose: dog	●	●		●			●	●	●		●	●	
Rose: guelder	●	●		●			●	●	●				
Sallow: common	●	●	●	●			●						
Willow: goat	●	●	●	●		●	●						

* 1 – well-drained loam; 2 – poorly drained clay/silt; 3 – waterlogged clay/slit; 4 – poor clay; 5 – subsoil only; 6 – rubble; 7 – rubble/soil mix; 8 – exposed sites; 9 – atmospheric pollution; 10 – unburnt shale; 11 – burnt shale/very dry soil; 12 – ash; 13 – lime waste.

Note: Many of the plants will grow in a wider range of conditions than those listed, e.g. almost all of them will do well on a good loam. The table indicates the sites where they can be used to best advantage.

(Source: Emery, 1986)

advance planning is particularly important for woodland habitat. Unless it is a bare earth site, make as much use of what is already there as you can. Simply accelerate and guide natural succession.

For conservation and amenity woodland, it is usual to plant a mixture of species. These are best planted in small groups of the same type to avoid a haphazard, spotted, or over-regimented appearance. Where different species are planted together at random, the more vigorously growing ones may take over. Adjacent groups should be chosen so that they produce an attractive blend of shape and colour, with the effect of seasonal changes kept in mind.

Block planting and straight lines should be avoided. Curved edges, linked with the topography and other features of the site, generally look more pleasing and natural. If a regular formal pattern of planting is necessary to simplify the task for those doing the work, an asymmetrical stagger can be used instead of a rectangular grid (see Figure 6.1).

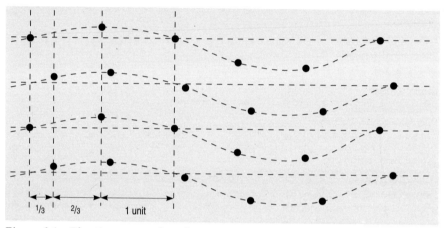

Figure 6.1 Planting pattern based on asymmetrically staggered rows (Source: Emery, 1986)

Spacing depends on the size of the planting stock, which can vary from between 0.2 and 1.2 metres tall for **transplants** to more than 3.5 metres for **extra heavy standards**. Transplants and **whips** nearly always survive better than larger plants except in heavily used areas, such as parks and playing fields, where they may be trampled. They are cheaper, easier to handle and grow faster than standards. In urban situations and for amenity purposes trees and shrubs are often planted very densely in order to produce an immediate effect. For example, trees can be planted as close as 1 metre apart, and shrubs 0.45 metres apart, and then thinned or coppiced before they become overcrowded, about 5 years later. Dense planting helps suppress weeds and protects individual trees from wind damage and vandalism. More conventional tree spacing, at 2 metres apart for transplants, allows the chance for other tree species to be recruited naturally and delays the need for thinning by about a further 10 years.

Once the shape and size of the scrub or woodland has been decided, and the mixture of species, planting pattern, and size and spacing of plants chosen, a detailed plan should be drawn and the number of plants required calculated. If stock is to be purchased, it is best ordered well in advance of planting to ensure that enough plants of the right size and type will be available when required.

Plants can be purchased from local garden centres, tree nurseries (often advertised in horticultural journals), the Forestry Commission, and many local authorities. The plants should be sturdy and well shaped, with a healthy main stem and leading shoot and a well-developed fibrous root system.

In some cases you may be able to use self-set saplings collected from a nearby site, providing the owner has given permission and removal does not interfere with natural regeneration of existing habitat. Establishment may be less successful than for nursery stock, which has usually been treated to withstand the planting procedure by annual transplanting to help build up a compact root ball.

You can also grow plants from seed or cuttings. Although this is more time-consuming it can be rewarding and educational. Members of the local community may like to help raise plants. Fallen seed can be collected from trees such as oak and beech, but other seeds may need to be harvested from the tree by using long-handled tools. If possible, seed should be collected locally and from sites with similar conditions to the new site. The landowner's permission should be sought before seed is taken.

Guidance on the collection, storage and sowing of seeds of different tree and shrub species is given in Table 6.3 (overleaf). As this shows, some seeds need a period of **stratification** to break dormancy. This involves keeping them moist and cool so that they slowly take up water until dormancy is broken. During this period the seeds need to be protected from mice and other seed eaters. This can be done by constructing a stratification pit, lined with wooden boards and wire mesh as shown in Figure 6.2. A layer of sharp sand or gravel is used to provide a free-draining base and the pit is then filled with a mixture of sand and seed in the proportion of four to one. The surface of the pit should be protected

Internal widths and depth of pit = 750 x 750 x 750mm

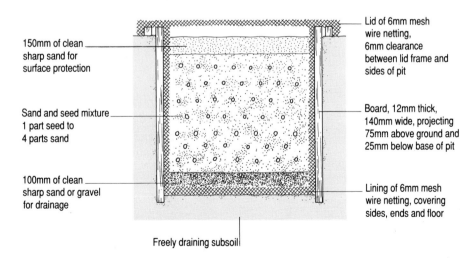

150mm of clean sharp sand for surface protection

Sand and seed mixture 1 part seed to 4 parts sand

100mm of clean sharp sand or gravel for drainage

Freely draining subsoil

Lid of 6mm mesh wire netting, 6mm clearance between lid frame and sides of pit

Board, 12mm thick, 140mm wide, projecting 75mm above ground and 25mm below base of pit

Lining of 6mm mesh wire netting, covering sides, ends and floor

Figure 6.2   Vertical cross-section of a stratification pit (Source: Emery 1986, after Aldhous, 1975)

Notes: (a) All woodwork should be treated with a copper-based preservative. Creosote must not be used, as it may harm seeds close to the boards;
(b) corner posts of the pit may be made from hard wood or angle iron driven well in. Boards must extend into the corners, those on the ends of the pit lapping the ends of the boards on the sides.

Table 6.3 Collection, storage and sowing of seeds of different tree and shrub species

Species	Collection	Stratification*	Sowing†
Trees			
Alder	Sept/Oct/Nov. Pick cones shortly before they ripen	–	Damp, not waterlogged soil; 10 mm deep; 10 g/sq m (35)
Ash	Sept/Oct/Nov. (Aug for sowing immediately). Seeds must be dry when collected	16–18	2nd spring; 60 g/sq m (70)
Beech	Aug/Oct/Nov. Free from husks before sowing. Can be sown immediately	–	Mar–Apr; 0.25 kg/sq m (60)
Birches	July/Aug/Sept. Pick catkins shortly before they ripen. Can be sown immediately	6	Mar–Apr; 5 g/sq m (40)
Blackthorn	Oct. Pick ripe berries	6 or 18	1st/2nd spring; 25–30 mm deep
Broom	Aug. Pick pods when black. Pop open by hand	–	Mar–Apr; 8 g/sq m (80)
Cherries	July/Sept/Oct. Pick ripe berries before birds do. Sow immediately, or dry and store in open containers	4	Mar–Apr; 150 g/sq m (80)
Crab apple	Sept/Oct. Pick from tree. Avoid rotten or scabby fruit	2	Jan; 10–25 mm deep; in sunny position
Hornbeam	Aug/Sept/Nov. Pick ripe seed before seed heads break up. Plant germinated seeds immediately	18	2nd spring; 5–10 mm deep; 60 g/sq m (45)
Limes	Oct. May be collected from the ground	18	2nd spring; up to 50 mm deep, 25–40 mm apart; 50 g/sq m (small–leaved); 200 g/sq m (large–leaved) (70)
Maple: field	Sept–Oct. Some seed most years. Can be sown immediately	18	2nd spring; 40 g/sq m
Mountain ash	July/Aug/Sept. Pick fully ripe berries. Store in open container	6–24	5 mm deep; 50 g/sq m (70)
Oaks	Sept/Oct/Nov. Collect from ground. Free acorns from cups	–	Mar–Apr; singly; 1 kg/sq m (80)
White poplar	Apr–May. Collect catkins when white down appears. Sow immediately	–	Apr–May; difficult to grow
Whitebeam	Aug/Sept/Oct. Pick fully ripe berries	6–24	5 mm deep; 50 g/sq m
Woodland edge /scrub			
Dog rose	Sept. Remove seeds from hips	7	Apr; 5–10 mm deep
Dogwood	Sept/Oct. Can be stratified whole	6	Mar–Apr; 5–10 mm deep
Elder	Aug/Sept. Collect as soon as ripe	6 or 18	1st/2nd spring; 5 mm deep
Guelder rose	Sept/Oct. Collect soon after fruiting	12	Sept–Oct; 5–10 mm deep
Hawthorns	Sept/Oct/Nov. Pick fully ripe berries. Can be stratified whole	18	2nd spring; 5 mm deep; 100g/sq m
Hazel	Sept/Oct. May be picked from the ground or when husks begin to brown	3–4	Apr; singly, 25–40 mm apart; up to 50 mm deep; 0.5 kg/sq m (80)
Holly	Nov/Dec/Jan. Pick when ripe. Stratify whole	16	2nd spring; 5–10 mm deep; 30 g/sq m (80)

* Stratification refers to stratification period in months. Seeds of broom need to be soaked in boiling water to break their dormancy. Seed contained in a fleshy fruit can be separated by soaking in warm water and gently mashing.

† Average per cent germination is given in parentheses where known.

(Source: Emery, 1986)

with a mesh cover. Small amounts of seed can be stratified by mixing them with moist sand and storing them in a plastic bag in a refrigerator or in a mouse-proof box in a cool shed.

The seeds can be sown directly into the woodland site or established first by sowing the seed in a well-tilled and sheltered nursery bed. It is important to ensure that the seeds are kept moist, so they should be sown deeper on lighter soils. Autumn sowing is usually more successful than sowing in the spring, especially where the spring tends to be dry. A covering of mulch helps conserve soil moisture and protect the seeds from being eaten. Acorns can be very successfully sown directly into a site if a tree tube is erected around each one to protect it and promote growth.

Many shrubs and trees can be reproduced by vegetative propagation, as well as from seed. Methods of vegetative propagation include taking cuttings (using cut shoots, each with a bud, from the parent plant), layering (illustrated in Chapter 5), or using **suckers** (woody upright shoots arising from shallow roots).

Planting out

If a wood with a mixture of shrubs, trees and herbaceous plants is planned, it is best to establish the shrubs and any shade-sensitive trees (such as oak) first. All the shrubs and any understorey trees will need to be shade-tolerant unless they are to be planted at the woodland edge. The planting of woodland grasses, flowers and climbers is best left until conditions become shady and moist as the tree canopy begins to close.

Shrubs and deciduous broadleaved trees should be planted over the winter, while they are dormant, preferably between mid-October and early December when the soil is still likely to be relatively warm and moist. Frosty spells should be avoided. Although container-grown plants can be planted out at any time of year, winter planting is least damaging to the roots. Evergreens, such as holly and most conifers, are best planted under moist conditions in early spring.

The time between lifting and planting should be kept to a minimum. It is essential to protect the roots from damage and from drying out. To protect plants in transit, the roots can be wrapped in damp straw in a plastic bag. If bad weather or other factors delay planting, bare-rooted plants can be stored in temporary trenches, with their roots covered in soil. Plants with the root ball wrapped in hessian or plastic, or container-grown, should be kept well ventilated and shaded to avoid overheating the roots. In the winter, they may need to be stored in trenches to prevent the soil and roots from freezing.

Small transplants can be planted by opening up a slot in the ground with a spade, a method termed **notch planting**. For larger plants individual pits need to be dug. The pits should be sufficiently large to allow a clearance of about 30 centimetres all round the root ball and 25 centimetres below. Pit planting may not succeed on compacted sites since the pit can become, in effect, a container full of water that drowns the tree. Trees should be planted so that ground level matches the original soil height on the stem. Compost or other organic material can be added to the soil where site conditions are poor, and the incorporation of some fertiliser is usually recommended to aid rapid establishment, although it can also promote vigorous weed growth. The soil around the roots should be firmed by gentle treading during planting and more heavily trodden down once planting is complete.

Provided well-rooted plants are used and planting is done in the winter, few trees should be lost to drought. Weeding is more crucial than watering to tree survival and growth. A mulch of coarse chopped bark or black plastic sheeting (or old plastic sack) helps conserve soil moisture and keeps down weeds. If a mulch is not used, the area immediately around each tree should be regularly scraped clear of weeds or treated with herbicide for at least the first few years wherever feasible.

Intensive maintenance for the first 3 to 5 years, including thorough weeding, fertiliser use and irrigation, can be used to accelerate tree growth. On the other hand, most trees planted with care will survive with little maintenance, although growth will initially be slow.

Tree guards or fencing may be needed where grazing by rabbits, hares, deer or livestock is a problem. Larger trees may need to be supported by loosely tying them to short stakes on exposed sites. If ties are needed, use proprietary brands and ensure that the tie is removed once the tree is established.

Planting hedges

Hedges can be useful as barriers on a new site, as well as looking attractive and providing valuable habitat. As in the creation of other habitat types, wild species that are known to do well locally should be used. Hawthorn and blackthorn are more robust than beech or hornbeam. Other species such as holly, guelder rose, privet, dogwood, wayfaring tree, field maple, hazel and crab apple can be used in small numbers to add variety and colour to the main hedging species.

The proposed site of the hedge can be prepared by ploughing, rotovating or digging the soil to a depth of 30 centimetres where site conditions permit. The plants can be set 20–45 centimetres apart, or 10 centimetres apart for a dense hedge, in either a single or a double staggered row. The young hedge may need to be surrounded by a fence at first to ensure that it is not inadvertently trampled on, and to protect it from rabbits if it is on a green wedge or urban fringe site. Heavy pruning can be used on planting to encourage bushy growth. The soil around the shrubs should be kept free of competitive plants until the hedge is established (3 to 5 years). One way of achieving this is to plant the hedge through holes in a strip of black plastic sheeting.

6.5   Creating aquatic habitats

Ponds and marshy areas can be among the most rewarding of habitats to create since they rapidly accumulate a rich variety of wildlife, as well as providing drinking and bathing places for birds and other animals from elsewhere. Constant wildlife activity in and around water makes a pond a fascinating area to watch and study, and the presence of water enlivens a landscape and provides an attractive feature. However, a pond requires a lot of maintainance and, if lined, is susceptible to inadvertent damage as well as vandalism on heavily used sites.

Siting a new pond

The most obvious requirement determining the site of a new pond is a source of unpolluted water. If the site is not naturally wet and there is no watercourse nearby from which water could be abstracted, tap water can be used although it is not ideal since it is treated with chlorine. If tap water has to be used to fill a pond, a minimum of two days should be allowed before aquatic wildlife is introduced, to allow time for the chlorine to clear. Where a pond is kept topped up with tap water, a separate 'feeder' pond can be constructed in which the tap water is temporarily stored before being allowed into the main pond.

The water level will be more easily maintained if the pond is sited on low flat ground where run-off will collect naturally. Rain that falls on adjoining land can be channelled to the pond by installing drains or diverting those that already exist. Rainwater can also be piped from the roofs of any buildings nearby. A trap may be needed at the water inlet to prevent silt and oil entering the pond, and sites near roads and car parks should be avoided to prevent this form of pollution. An outlet pipe may be needed to contain and direct any overflow.

The pond should preferably be in a position where it is clearly visible, both to ensure the safety of children and to discourage fly-tipping. It should be sited far enough away from existing trees to be protected from excessive leaf fall and heavy shading.

The presence of old building foundations, industrial waste and underground services may make excavation difficult in some places. If no more suitable situation can be found, it may still be possible to create a pond by mounding up the surrounding soil rather than by excavating the middle.

Designing a pond

The bigger the pond, the more stable the habitat will be for wildlife. A minimum area of 5 × 5 metres is preferable, with an average depth of 1–1.5 metres. By varying the depth of the pond and the slopes of its banks, conditions can be created to suit a wide range of plants and animals. Parts of the pond deeper than 0.75 metres provide greater protection from extremes of heat and cold, serving as refuges when there is a risk of the pond drying out or when the surface of the water is frozen. Beyond a depth of 2 metres little light penetrates and fewer organisms live so that there is little advantage to be gained from excavating more deeply.

Gently sloping banks allow a broad band of vegetation to develop at the water's margin, and are less hazardous than steep edges in places that are accessible to children. Since artificial pond liners deteriorate in sunlight, slopes of less than 1 in 3 are necessary to keep a protective covering of soil in place if a liner is used. On larger ponds, the creation of islands well away from the banks can provide areas free from disturbance for nesting birds. Marshy areas can be created by extending the lining of the pond to produce a shelf at the edge and covering it with subsoil or soil taken from an existing marshy area.

Constructing a pond

A pond can be constructed by taking advantage of naturally wet conditions on the site, or by using some form of impermeable lining to retain the water. The materials that can be used for lining a pond include **puddled clay**, flexible pond liners (such as butyl rubber), concrete or pre-shaped glass fibre.

The presence of springs, seepage lines or permanently wet ground all indicate a high water table or impermeable soil. Plants such as rushes, horsetails and meadowsweet are also indicative of wet ground. Ideally, the

Naturally wet conditions

suitability of the site for pond construction should be checked by digging test pits to the required depth and monitoring water levels throughout the year. If water levels are adequate, a pond can be constructed simply by excavating a hollow and using the excavated soil to form shallow sloping banks around the edge.

If water is to be diverted to the pond from an existing water course, this will need the approval of the National Rivers Authority (in England and Wales) or the River Purification Board (in Scotland) and professional help with the design. The water course may be fed directly into the pond (on-stream) or some of the water abstracted by means of a small diversion (off-stream).

Excavation

The production of a detailed scale diagram showing the planned contours of the pond, as shown in the example in Figure 6.3, can be a useful guide to excavation. The outline and main contours can be marked on the ground with stakes joined by string. If the stakes are marked at regular intervals, a simple water level can be used to show when the banks are at the same height (see Figure 6.4).

Where groundwater levels are low, some form of impermeable lining is necessary to construct a pond. To provide a rough estimate of the quantity of pond lining required, the width and length of the excavated area should be

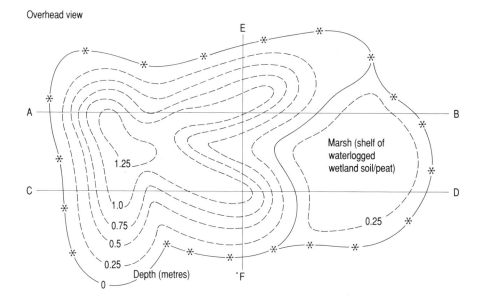

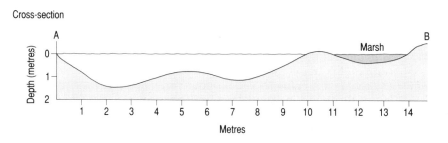

Figure 6.3 Plan for a pond

98

Equipment: A length of garden hose, at least 5m longer than the pool is wide, and two pieces of open-ended transparent tubing to fit on each end

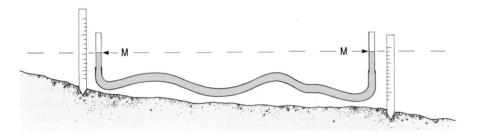

M = Meniscus – when the hose is filled with water until visible in both transparent tubes, the water will always settle at its own level. No matter how the hose lies in the hole, the height of the water in the tube will be the same at both ends, so that an imaginary line running between will always be horizontal. The height of the water in each tube may be compared to marked stakes, set in the ground at the edges of the hole, to gauge the level of the ground or pond banks

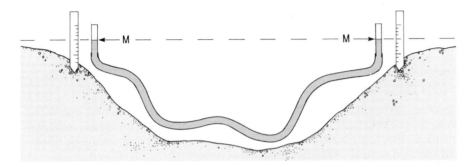

Figure 6.4 A simple water level

measured by running a tape down one bank, along the bottom, and up the other side. Alternatively, the distances can be estimated from similar measurements taken from accurate cross-sectional drawings of the pond, using a piece of string. For artificial pond liners, 1 metre should be added all round to the measurements to allow for the overlap needed at the edge. If the pond is to be lined with a layer of clay, the amount of clay needed can be calculated by multiplying the width and length (with 1 metre added all round as a safety margin) by the depth of clay required (normally about 25 centimetres). Since the raw clay is compressed during pond construction this must be taken into account in the calculation, as follows:

Amount of clay required (in cubic metres, if all measurements are in metres)

= (length + 1 m) × (width + 1 m) × (final depth of clay) × 1.3.

Puddled clay is the traditional form of pond lining. Puddling involves spreading clay onto a smooth, stone-free surface, wetting the clay, and trampling it, or compacting it with a tractor, until it becomes solid and plastic. The puddled clay is built up in layers, a few centimetres at a time, until a minimum consolidated depth of 20 centimetres is reached. The puddled clay must be kept moist at all times or it can develop cracks that are difficult to seal. If construction has to be halted for any reason, the lining should be temporarily flooded. Frost can also crack the clay, so that puddling should not be done when frosty conditions are likely. Because of the risk of cracking, clay lining is unsuitable where water levels are likely to fluctuate.

Clay lining

For large-scale projects, such as reservoirs, and for repairs to existing ponds, Bentonite clay is sometimes used. This is a fine-powdered clay that swells to 15 times its original volume when wetted. It is mixed with soil to form an impermeable lining. It is much more expensive than ordinary clay but less susceptible to cracking.

Flexible pond liners

Sheets of polyvinyl chloride (PVC) or butyl rubber are a popular form of lining for small ponds. Since they are gradually degraded by sunlight, they need to be covered with a layer of soil or other protective material. As already mentioned, this means that the contours of the pond must be gently sloping, rather than steep, to retain the covering in place. Flexible pond liners should not be used in wet ground as the surrounding water pressure can cause them to lift.

The hollow to be lined should be smooth and free of sharp stones, with firm banks and sides to prevent loose soil slipping and stressing the liner. A layer of sand or similar protection (turves, fine ash, sawdust, newspaper, old carpets or proprietary fibre matting) should be spread to form the base on which the liner is laid. The liner can be secured in place by digging a shallow trench around the edge of the pond, laying the liner loosely over this and filling the trench back up with soil. Clayey soil should be used to encase the edge of the liner in the trench since porous soil can act as a wick and siphon off water from the pond. The whole liner should then be protected with a 10 centimetre layer of stone-free soil. Additional protection, such as fibre matting or burying the liner under a much deeper layer of soil, is advisable if heavy use (for example by children pond-dipping) is anticipated.

Concrete

Concrete can be used as a lining for small ponds but is liable to crack unless the lining is on a firm base, very well constructed and thick. Since cement contains chemicals that are toxic to wildlife, a new concrete-lined pond should be filled and emptied several times over a period of a month before it is used.

Glass fibre

Pre-shaped glass fibre ponds are expensive and not recommended except for small projects, such as in school playgrounds or gardens. Those with shallow sloping sides and underwater ledges provide the most scope for wildlife.

Introducing aquatic wildlife

Aquatic plants

Aquatic plants help oxygenate the water and counter the harmful effects of water pollution. As with other habitats, introduced plants should be those most suited to the conditions and ideally locally typical. Many garden centres now stock a variety of aquatic species, but invasive species such as Canadian pondweed should be avoided. Local wildlife trusts may be able to recommend sources of supply. Local authorities and local water companies may be able to provide information about water courses being dredged or cleared of vegetation that could provide a source of plants. Permission should be sought from the owner before collecting plants from other sites.

Submerged aquatics are those plants that grow almost wholly underwater, such as spiked water-milfoil, common water crowfoot, and curled, perfoliate, various-leaved and fennel pondweeds. Some are highly invasive in the absence of competition so several species should be introduced at the same time with the aim of establishing separate blocks.

Floating-leaved, rooted aquatics are plants that root in the bottom mud of the pond but have leaves that float on the water surface. They include water lilies (white, yellow and fringed) and broad-leaved pondweed. As with submerged aquatics, it is a good idea to introduce several types at one time so that no one species becomes dominant. In small ponds their growth may need to be checked to avoid shading out submerged plants, or they can be planted in baskets to prevent them spreading.

Emergent aquatics grow in shallow water. Examples include water horsetail, lesser spearwort, watercress, amphibious bistort, water plantain, flowering rush, bur-reed, great reedmace (bulrush), lesser reedmace, common reed and reed canary grass. Reedmace and common reed can be very invasive and should be avoided in small ponds. Where invasive species are used, several should be planted at the same time in blocks, sited where they can be easily reached if their growth needs to be checked.

Marginal plants grow in marshy ground near the water's edge. They include marsh marigold, brooklime, bogbean, water forget-me-not, water mint, rushes, yellow flag and some sedges.

Trees that flourish near water include alder, black poplar and willows. Bankside trees provide valuable cover for birds, but they are best restricted to the northern side to avoid shading the water. As already mentioned, they should not be planted where the roots might damage the pond lining or drains.

Aquatic animals often find their own way to water as eggs attached to the leaves of introduced plants or in the mud around their roots. The adult forms of many aquatic invertebrates are winged and so easily spread from nearby ponds and watercourses; examples include dragonflies, damselflies, mayflies, caddis flies, stoneflies and water beetles.

Aquatic animals

If necessary, mud from other well-stocked ponds and watercourses can be used as a source of aquatic animals. Snails are particularly valuable pond inhabitants since they help keep the water free of excessive growths of algae. Frog spawn can be transferred from areas where there is plenty or that are likely to dry out, but advice should be sought before transferring less common amphibians. Taking spawn of the great crested newt is illegal. The introduction of fish can profoundly disturb a pond's ecosystem, for example many fish eat the larvae of newts, so is not recommended for small ponds. A licence may be needed to transfer fish from another water body; this can be obtained from the National Rivers Authority (in England and Wales) or the Scottish Office, Agriculture and Fisheries Department (in Scotland).

6.6   *Small-scale wildlife features*

It is not necessary to have large areas devoted to habitat in order to attract wildlife. Window boxes and flower borders can provide nectar, pollen and seeds. Small trees, shrubs, hedges, and climbing plants against walls and fences provide nesting cover and berries. Miniature wildflower meadows can be created in garden lawns or in the mown grass that often surrounds housing estates and lines pavements. Bird tables, bird baths, nesting boxes, hedgehog boxes and garden ponds can all be used to encourage wildlife. Woodpiles, compost heaps and a weedy corner where wild plants such as nettles are left provide additional habitat.

You don't really need a BTCV work party Mr Archer — try a drop of water!

Small areas of wildlife habitat can add interest to all types of urban sites that are used mainly for leisure and recreation. The example in Figure 6.5 (overleaf) shows how the layout of allotments on a site in Birmingham has been redesigned to incorporate wildlife features.

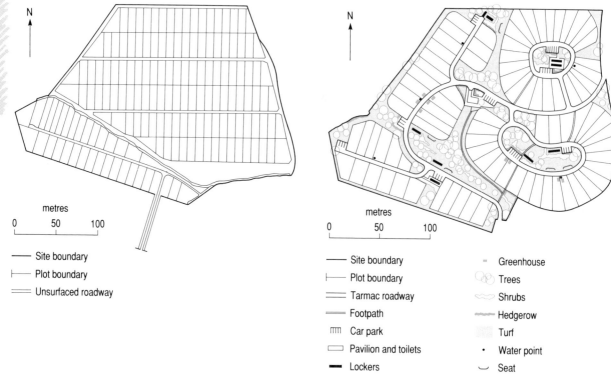

N

N

metres

0   50   100

—— Site boundary

├— Plot boundary

══ Unsurfaced roadway

metres

0   50   100

—— Site boundary   ═ Greenhouse

├— Plot boundary   ◯◯ Trees

══ Tarmac roadway   ～ Shrubs

══ Footpath   ▬ Hedgerow

▥ Car park   ▦ Turf

▭ Pavilion and toilets · Water point

▬ Lockers   ⌣ Seat

Figure 6.5   Redesign of allotments in Birmingham, to create a community leisure garden with considerable additional areas of wildlife habitat (Source: Gilbert, 1991)

6.7   Exercise 6: Designing new habitat areas

1   Check through the options described in this chapter for any that apply to your chosen site.

2   Add any options you select to your sketch map and work plan.

6.8   Case study example of creating a new habitat

Brandon Hill Nature Park

The 2 hectare Brandon Hill Nature Park occupies a prominent position only 0.5 kilometres from Bristol's city centre, close to large populations of both residents and commuters. Formerly a traditional Victorian park, the site has been developed by Avon Wildlife Trust as a wildlife area as a result of a proposal they submitted to the City Council in a competition for ideas to improve Bristol.

One consideration that may have influenced the Council's decision in favour of the Trust's idea was the site's steep slopes, which made mowing technically difficult. As a result, small patches of scrub and the occasional tree had become established along the lower slopes of the park. Elsewhere the site presented the Trust with a plain green grassy canvas on which to set out their design (see Figure 6.6).

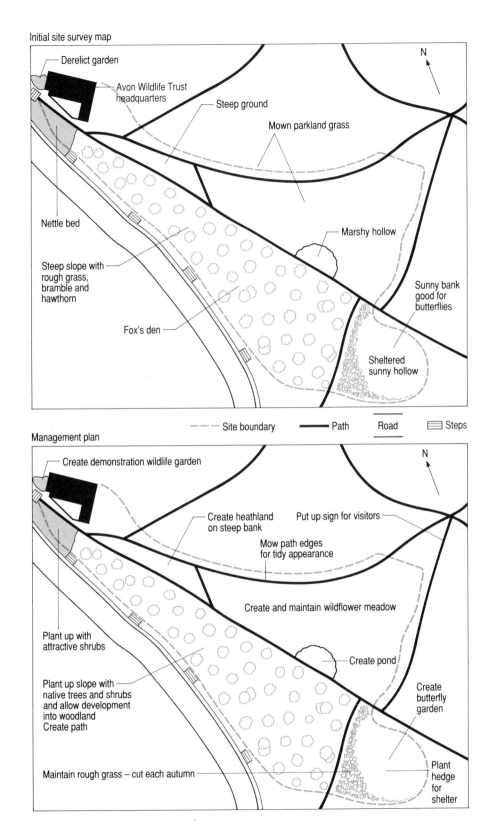

Initial site survey map

Derelict garden

Avon Wildlife Trust headquarters

Steep ground

Mown parkland grass

N

Nettle bed

Marshy hollow

Steep slope with rough grass, bramble and hawthorn

Sunny bank good for butterflies

Fox's den

Sheltered sunny hollow

- - - Site boundary   —— Path   Road   ▤ Steps

Management plan

Create demonstration wildlife garden

Create heathland on steep bank

Put up sign for visitors

Mow path edges for tidy appearance

N

Create and maintain wildflower meadow

Plant up with attractive shrubs

Plant up slope with native trees and shrubs and allow development into woodland Create path

Create pond

Create butterfly garden

Maintain rough grass – cut each autumn

Plant hedge for shelter

Figure 6.6   Brandon Hill Nature Park

The Trust's main objectives for the nature park were twofold:

▶ to create examples of typical local habitats in an urban situation for everyone to enjoy;

▶ to demonstrate how wildlife can be attracted and encouraged to an urban site.

There were two main constraints that influenced the design and management of the site.

▶ The gradients across most of the site are too steep to use machinery, and cannot readily be reformed. This prevented the creation of wetland habitats apart from one small pond, and the other habitat boundaries were largely dictated by the gradient.

▶ The public's perception of a park, at least when the project began, was of a tidy, functional and formal area with mown grass and the occasional tree. This inhibited the Trust from trying out drastic techniques such as removing the topsoil from the meadow area; it has also meant that a much greater emphasis has been placed on tidiness than in a typical nature reserve.

In addition, limits on available resources have inevitably slowed down the development of some projects. Most of the costs of running the park have been met by the Trust, who have had to raise funds for specific projects. Big businesses have helped considerably with sponsorship, no doubt attracted by the park's central location and innovative design.

The nature park has now been established for over 10 years. It has two major habitats (secondary woodland/scrub, and a hay meadow), three minor habitats (a pond, heathland and grassy glades), and a demonstration butterfly border and pocket-sized wildlife garden.

Most of the really steep slopes have been planted with trees and shrubs, so enhancing the existing hawthorn and bramble scrub. The semi-mature sycamore and turkey oaks scattered across the lower slopes have been left since they provide the basic structure of a woodland and are appreciated by the public. The long-term objective is to favour species of greater benefit to wildlife. Some grassy glades have been retained. Bluebell and daffodil bulbs have been planted where the ground flora is sparse.

Although historically Brandon Hill has harboured a range of small herbs associated with species-rich acid grasslands, these have not reappeared in the nature park probably because the soils are too deep. The sward that the Trust inherited was dominated by false oat-grass, Yorkshire fog, bents and ribwort plantain. A range of techniques has been used by the Trust to try and increase the plant diversity of the grassland. A hay crop has been taken from the area each year in late July in the hope that this will reduce the nutrient status of the soil and thus the vigour of the grasses. Only where the soils are a little thinner does this seem to have happened.

The use of wildflower seed mixes has proved unsuccessful. Several metre square plots were stripped of turf and then seeded, but in almost every case they were taken over by species that were already prevalent, such as dandelions and ribwort plantain. The introduction of herb-rich turf from sites that were about to be lost to development has allowed a few extra species to establish, although in every case the original diversity of the transplanted turf has greatly diminished.

The most successful technique for increasing the sward diversity has been the introduction of individual pot-grown plants. Tall herbs such as ox-eye daisy, black knapweed and devil's-bit scabious have been used because of the height of the sward. Most of these plants have persisted, and at last parts of the meadow now capture the colour of a traditional hay meadow.

The pond

The pond is undoubtedly the visitors' favourite feature, especially in the spring when amphibians are most active. The pond was fenced early on as this proved the only way of keeping out hot, thirsty dogs! The fence seems to have increased people's curiosity as well as their respect for the pond. Apart from dogs, another problem has been the all too common one of accidentally introduced and invasive plants such as Canadian pondweed. Unfortunately, the pond lacks any natural water source and tends to dry out in summer. While this is obviously a natural process, an area of wet mud is not the most effective medium for conveying the delights of wildlife to the public!

The heathland

The Trust tried transplanting some species-rich heathland, from yet another doomed site, on to a small steep bank. This was unsuccessful. All the heather and bilberry died back after only 12 months, while coarse grasses have steadily swamped the herb component in the turf transplants. It is technically quite difficult to transplant turves deep enough to support typical heathland shrubs. In addition, although Brandon Hill is underlain with sandstone, the clayey topsoil is probably not suitable for heathland plants.

Accommodating visitors

During the initial development of the project in particular it proved essential to maintain the edges of the paths to give the impression of a cared-for site, in order to conform with people's preconceptions of a public park. This has proved less important along the new footpath running through the woodland area, presumably because there was no previously established use in this area.

Large interpretative signs are used to explain what is going on but do not seem to encourage anyone other than the enthusiast to explore the nooks and crannies of the site. The park is still mainly visited on route from A to B or as part of a lunchtime stroll rather than to explore its wildlife. The exhibition centre in the Trust's headquarters next to the site is little used, possibly because it is at the far end of the park away from the main entrance.

Community involvement

Despite occasional door-to-door leaflets and posters advertising volunteer workdays, virtually no local residents have shown any interest in becoming involved in the project. The more formal features in the nature park, such as the butterfly border and wildlife garden, need a lot of maintenance and it was assumed that keen amateur gardeners would volunteer to do most of this work. As this has not been the case, these features have often proved less than showpieces.

The Avon Wildlife Trust has learnt a great deal about habitat creation and urban conservation through its involvement with the nature park. In particular:

▶   Very public sites should be maintained to a high standard if urban conservation is to gain widespread credibility.

▶   Visually attractive interesting features are required to capture the public's imagination.

▶   The general public are still not demanding urban conservation measures and so the benefits need to be sold to incidental users of sites such as Brandon Hill.

(Source: Antony Merritt, Avon Wildlife Trust)

Chapter 7
PROMOTING AND INTERPRETING
URBAN HABITATS

As Case Study 6 suggests, the pleasure to be derived from encouraging wildlife in urban areas is not yet apparent to everyone. Active promotion and interpretation of urban wildlife sites is needed if people are to enjoy and appreciate them to the full. Urban sites provide the ideal opportunity to encourage a better understanding of wildlife and wildlife habitats, more widespread support for nature conservation and a greater respect for the environment as a whole.

Promotion involves increasing people's awareness of a site and encouraging its use by visitors. Most promotional activities take place away from the site. Their purpose is to let people know what they can expect to see and do there, by such means as leaflets, posters in local shops, libraries and community centres, and media coverage.

Interpretation involves explaining the significance of a site to those who visit it. Interpretation usually takes place on the site, by such means as signs, trail leaflets, guided tours, demonstrations, educational activities and displays.

Decisions about what type of promotion and interpretation is appropriate need to be closely linked to the characteristics of the site and the expected visitors. As with habitat management, a systematic approach to site promotion and interpretation, working to an overall plan, is likely to be most effective. A similar series of steps can be followed: assessment of the site's existing and potential use for visitors; definition of objectives and constraints; exploring and selecting options; drawing up a work plan; implementing the plan and monitoring progress.

You should find that you have already recorded most of the information you need during your original site assessment. At this stage you may simply need to consider it in greater detail and from a different perspective, that of the visitor.

7.1   Assessing a site's potential use by visitors

Each site differs in its potential for use by visitors, as the case studies throughout this book show. For example, the nature area set up by staff at Perkins Technology in Peterborough is on a privately controlled site, on the outskirts of the city, so that the main visitors are the company's own staff and sometimes their families. Open access is not a practical option. Even so, the company do have plans to encourage the site's use by local schools and community groups, and to use it to demonstrate to other companies what can be achieved at the workplace.

The Fens Pools site, which the Pensnett Wildlife Group help manage, is quite different. It is large, freely accessible, in a densely populated area and used for a variety of activities over which the group has little control. With the help of full-time wardens, a classroom on site, the support of the local authority, and a large number of enthusiastic and knowledgeable group members, a great variety of promotional and interpretative activities is possible.

The characteristics of a site that affect its use by visitors include:

▶ its size;

▶ its accessibility and terrain;

▶ legal considerations, such as form of ownership and tenancy agreements;

▶ any hazards to visitors;

▶ sensitivity of its habitats to disturbance;

▶ special features that might attract certain types of visitor;

▶ visitor facilities on the site;

▶ resources in terms of funding and people to help;

▶ management objectives for the site.

The characteristics of the visitors who already use or might be expected to use the site also need to be assessed, for example:

▶ how many visitors currently use the site and how many might be expected in response to site promotion;

▶ how far do visitors travel to the site and how do they get there (walk, cycle, bus, car);

▶ how often do they visit and how long do they stay;

▶ what do they appreciate, or dislike, about the site and what facilities would they like to see incorporated (refer back to Table 2.1 for ideas);

▶ what are their views on wildlife;

▶ what groups exist within the catchment of the site and might be targeted by promotional materials?

Some of this information can be obtained by holding group discussions with a representative group of local people. Brainstorming can be a useful way of generating new ideas about developing a site's use by visitors. For this, members of the group first spend some time putting forward as many opinions and ideas as possible, however far-fetched. The list of ideas is then discussed and modified as a basis for a set of practical proposals. Additional information can be gathered by observation of people on the site and by surveys conducted on the site or in local schools, shopping areas or community centres. Such surveys should be short and simple, and should not ask leading or ambiguous questions.

7.2   Promotion

This section provides a range of ideas and examples that you might like to consider for promoting your group and site, some of which overlap with interpretation. Not all will be relevant to every site, and you will probably come across many other ideas by observing how other people gain publicity, whatever their purpose.

It is worth bearing in mind that often sponsorship can be obtained for promotional material, as some of the examples show. If you can co-ordinate your promotional activities with those of other similar groups and sites in the area, for example by producing a series of leaflets covering all local wildlife sites, you are likely to achieve a higher profile.

General awareness of your group and what it is trying to achieve can be raised by public appeals for help with unusual or interesting projects. For example, in Brighton the urban wildlife group asked for help in mapping the distribution of hedgehogs locally; part of a completed hedgehog survey form is shown in Figure 7.1. A similar project in the Newcastle-under-Lyme and Potteries area invited residents to report owl sightings. In this case the response was not so good, possibly because owls are not so often seen. Again in Brighton, residents are invited to send in any dead bird or mammal they find to the local natural history museum, where the resident taxidermist prepares the specimens for wildlife displays and a school loans collection.

Similar public appeals might be used to collect old photographs and reminiscences of your site for publicity leaflets and displays, or to invite people to grow wildflowers and trees from seed to be planted out on the site.

Staffordshire Wildlife Trust have promoted the work they do by obtaining sponsorship from developers to give people buying new houses a year's family membership of the trust, a bird or bat box, a packet of wildflower seed and a book on wildlife gardening.

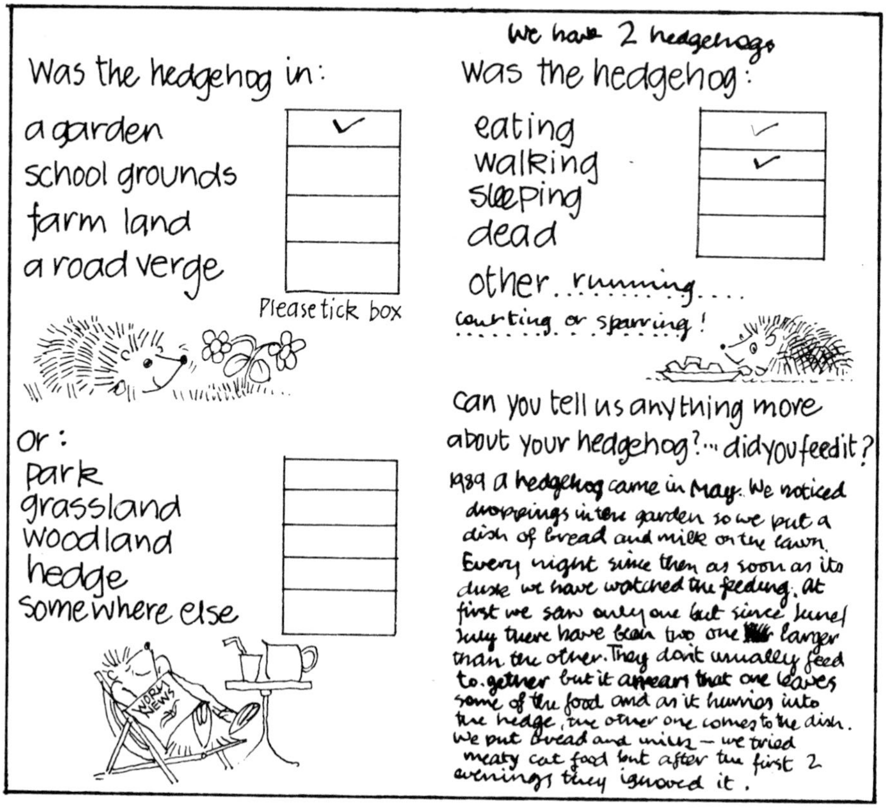

Figure 7.1   Part of a completed hedgehog survey form

More conventional methods of gaining publicity for sites include: delivering leaflets to houses; providing leaflets and posters for display in schools, shops, libraries, tourist information offices and community centres; issuing press releases and providing photographs and photo-opportunities for the media; mounting displays at libraries, local shows and fêtes; organising special events; giving talks to local groups and organisations; contributing articles to local magazines; and targeting particular groups of the community.

Often site management activities, such as litter clearing, tree planting and pond restoration, can be stage-managed to attract media attention and local interest, especially if a local dignatory or personality can be persuaded to inaugurate the proceedings. Imaginative events can be organised to encourage public participation; for example, a guided urban wildlife safari, a dawn chorus walk, a bat walk at dusk with electronic bat detectors, demonstrations of wildlife gardening or of woodcrafts such as charcoal production.

Publicity material about the site needs to give clear instructions about how to get there and information about the facilities available, as in the introduction to a leaflet about Crabtree Pond in Sheffield in Figure 7.2

Some groups of people may need to be specifically targeted to encourage and enable them to use a site, for example those who are house-bound, such as some women from minority ethnic groups, disabled people and older people. Liaison with social services and community workers may help identify such groups and any special needs or interests that they may have. Often help with transport is appreciated, and might be provided by a local sponsor.

Schools also may need to be encouraged to use a site and they too may need help with transport. Teachers may lack confidence in field study methods and may welcome advice and support. Even if they are familiar with field studies, they may not have experience of urban systems. They will need to know what is to be found on the site so that they can answer pupils' questions. They will also want information about the facilities available, for example parking, toilets, someone to talk to about the site. Some teachers may have their own activities planned but others will welcome suggestions,

WALKS ON THE WILD SIDE

A SERIES OF SELF-GUIDED NATURE WALKS THROUGH URBAN SHEFFIELD

1.   CRABTREE POND & ROE WOODS

The starting point for this walk is the junction of Barnsley Road (A6135) and Crabtree Close, Sheffield 5. At the time of writing (March 1991), the following buses stop nearby: 45, 46, 47, 48,75, 76, M46, 165 (stop on Barnsley Road) 97, 8/9, 22 (stop on Norwood Road). The first section of the walk, around Crabtree pond, has fairly good access for wheelchair users. At present, the other sections are pretty much inaccessible to people with restricted mobility, although there are plans to upgrade these paths in the near future. There are no toilet facilities along the route.

Figure 7.2   Part of a leaflet about Crabtree Pond and Roe Woods

especially if these can be linked to curriculum requirements. Illustrations that can be photocopied, such as site maps and background material may be helpful. If you plan to produce a resource pack, consult teachers about what they would find most useful. A public display of pupils' work after a visit to the site, for example in a local library or shop window, can help raise local awareness of a site's value and potential. Figure 7.3 illustrates extracts from a leaflet for teachers describing the resources available at Benwell Nature Park in Newcastle.

7.3   Interpretation

Good interpretation involves not only thinking clearly about the message you want to convey, but trying to imagine yourself in the visitor's place, to think about what they are likely to notice and what will most interest them. To help with ideas, ask others involved with the site to imagine the same, or ask visitors for their initial impressions. Children are often particularly good at providing a fresh perspective. You may be surprised at the differences in how different people view a site.

The type of information you provide might cover:

▶   what can be seen on, and from, the site (including wildlife, geological and archaeological features, and built structures);

▶   the reasons for particular management practices;

▶   how the site relates to its urban surroundings and to other wildlife habitats in the area;

▶   the history of the site and its links with the community.

For casual visitors to a site and those who only stay briefly, the message must be clear and simple. For those who regularly use the site, or who visit it for educational purposes, more detailed information can be provided.

The ideal method of presenting information is to have someone on the site, available to talk to visitors and answer questions. A variety of other methods can be used, including:

▶   publications, such as leaflets;

▶   signs and signposts;

▶   posters, wall charts and murals;

▶   hides, trails and look-out points, combined with other media;

▶   listening posts with recorded information;

▶   audio cassette tapes, for use with portable cassette players;

▶   automatic slide displays and video cassettes;

▶   displays of artefacts, such as animal bones and rocks;

▶   scale models;

▶   live exhibits, for example in an aquarium.

Some of their advantages and disadvantages are shown in Table 7.1 (overleaf).

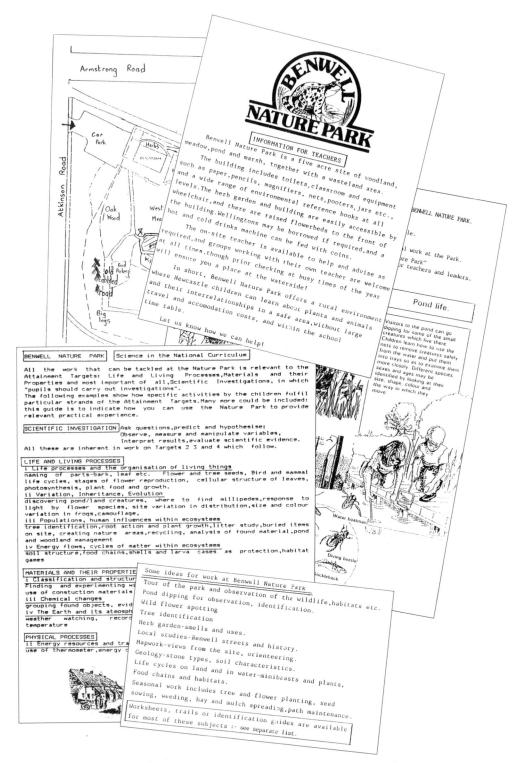

Map section (top left):

Armstrong Road

Atkinson Road

Car Park

Herbs

Oak Wood

West Mea

hot

Old Raleigh Road
Cobbled Road

Big logs

Information for Teachers leaflet:

BENWELL NATURE PARK

INFORMATION FOR TEACHERS

Benwell Nature Park is a five acre site of woodland, meadow,pond and marsh, together with a wasteland area.

The building includes toilets,classroom and equipment such as paper,pencils, magnifiers, nets,pooters,jars etc., and a wide range of environmental reference books at all levels.The herb garden and building are easily accessible by wheelchair,and there are raised flowerbeds to the front of the building.Wellingtons may be borrowed if required.The hot and cold drinks machine can be fed with coins.

The on-site teacher is available to help and advise as required,and groups working with their own teacher are welcome at all times,though prior checking at busy times of the year will ensure you a place at the waterside!

In short, Benwell Nature Park offers a rural environment where Newcastle children can learn about plants and animals and their interrelationships in a safe area,without large travel and accomodation costs, and within the school time table.

Let us know how we can help!

(Partly hidden leaflet, right):

BENWELL NATURE PARK.

...le.

...l work at the Park.

...re Park"

...r teachers and leaders.

Pond life.

Visitors to the pond can go dipping for some of the small creatures which live there. Children learn how to use the nets to remove creatures safely from the water and put them into trays so as to examine them more closely. Different species, sexes and ages may be identified by looking at their size, shape, colour and the way in which they move

Water boatman

Diving beetle

Stickleback

Science leaflet:

| BENWELL NATURE PARK | Science in the National Curriculum |

All the work that can be tackled at the Nature Park is relevant to the Attainment Targets: Life and Living Processes,Materials and their Properties and most important of all,Scientific Investigations, in which "pupils should carry out investigations".
The following examples show how specific activities by the children fulfil particular strands of the Attainment Targets.Many more could be included: this guide is to indicate how you can use the Nature Park to provide relevant practical experience.

SCIENTIFIC INVESTIGATION Ask questions,predict and hypothesise:
Observe, measure and manipulate variables,
Interpret results,evaluate scientific evidence.
All these are inherent in work on Targets 2 3 and 4 which follow.

LIFE AND LIVING PROCESSES
i Life processes and the organisation of living things
naming of parts-bark, leaf etc. Flower and tree seeds, Bird and mammal life cycles, stages of flower reproduction, cellular structure of leaves, photosynthesis, plant food and growth.
ii Variation, Inheritance, Evolution
discovering pond/land creatures, where to find millipedes,response to light by flower species, site variation in distribution,size and colour variation in frogs,camouflage,
iii Populations, human influences within ecosystems
tree identification,root action and plant growth,litter study,buried items on site, creating nature areas,recycling, analysis of found material,pond and woodland management
iv Energy flows, cycles of matter within ecosystems
soil structure,food chains,shells and larva cases as protection,habitat games

MATERIALS AND THEIR PROPERTIE...
i Classification and structur...
Finding and experimenting wi...
use of constuction materials ...
iii Chemical changes
grouping found objects, evid...
iv The Earth and its atmosph...
weather watching, record...
temperature

PHYSICAL PROCESSES
ii Energy resources and tra...
use of thermometer,energy ...

"Some ideas" leaflet:

Some ideas for work at Benwell Nature Park

Tour of the park and observation of the wildlife,habitats etc.
Pond dipping for observation, identification.
Wild flower spotting
Tree identification
Herb garden-smells and uses.
Local studies-Benwell streets and history.
Mapwork-views from the site, orienteering.
Geology-stone types, soil characteristics.
Life cycles on land and in water-minibeasts and plants.
Food chains and habitats.
Seasonal work includes tree and flower planting, seed sowing, weeding, hay and mulch spreading,path maintenance.

Worksheets, trails or identification guides are available for most of these subjects :- see separate list.

Figure 7.3   Extracts from a leaflet for teachers about Benwell Nature Park

Table 7.1 Advantages and disadvantages of different forms of site interpretation

Medium	Advantages	Disadvantages
Signs and panels	Can be the simplest and most cost-effective way to let passers-by know what is going on	Can distract attention from the site
	Allow people to help themselves to information if they want it	Can be an eyesore if inappropriate materials are used
	Well chosen graphics and words can convey a lot of information quickly and gain people's interest	Subject to vandalism
	Can provide information in more than one language if this would be useful to the local community	Can be expensive to update or replace
	Can enhance the appearance of the site if appropriate materials are used	Some do not last very long, particularly plastics and colours in sunlight
Leaflets and self-guided trails	Enable people to explore and find out about a site at their own pace	Theme leaflets can date, or be inappropriate to the season
	Can be a useful resource for a group leader of visitors to the site	
	Leaflets can be used for promotion as well as interpretation	
'Hands-on' artefacts and models	Can be very effective in getting a message across and in generating interest in a site	Usually need to be located indoors in an area such as a visitors' centre
Events	Can be very effective at raising awareness of site	Need a lot of organisation
	Provide an opportunity for people to get involved and to ask questions	Need advice on health and safety
	Provide an opportunity to find out from local visitors at first hand how they would like to be more involved	
	Can be very enjoyable for visitors and demonstrators	

The size and location of the site, the budget available, the information to be conveyed, the number of visitors, who they are and why they visit are among the factors that need to be considered when deciding on the most appropriate media. Where a few square metres of waste ground are to be sown with wildflower seed and supplied with a seat, a simple sign telling people what is being done may be all that is needed. Several hundred square metres of trees that need coppicing to improve their value for wildlife will need more explanation, possibly both by using an interpretative panel and by organising an event on the site. An old brick or gravel pit restored as a wetland site, complete with a visitors' centre, might provide opportunities for a wide range of activities, as well as audio-visual and interactive displays.

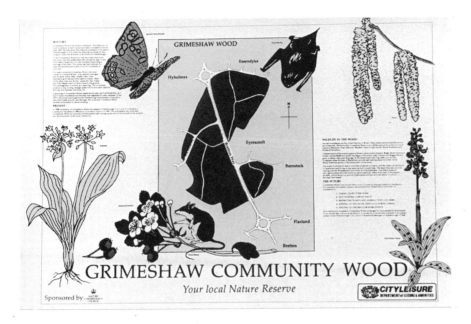

Figure 7.4   A well designed and welcoming entrance sign

A clearly visible and well designed sign at the entrance to the site, showing the site layout and what to look out for, is a simple way of making visitors feel welcome (see Figure 7.4 for an example).

The more you can get visitors' active involvement, the more information you can convey. Well-signposted nature trails, with signs or leaflets telling visitors what to look out for on route are one way of doing this. Work sheets with questions about the site for children to answer are another. The 'Look Out & About' booklets produced by the Pensnett Wildlife Group for all local primary schoolchildren provide an excellent example (see Figure 7.5 overleaf).

The type of events and activities mentioned under promotion can serve as a valuable form of interpretation as well as stimulating interest and involvement in a site. Most management activities have the potential to be used as demonstrations and as social occasions, with a picnic or barbecue on site to encourage participation.

Art, dance and street theatre linked to wildlife themes can help reach a wider audience. Examples include a mural depicting the story of how a derelict pond and its surrounds were turned into a nature garden, designed and painted by children at West Norwood Primary School in London; the dance project depicting the loss of a school's only tree in a storm, mentioned in Chapter 2; and a light-hearted sculpture of a swamp monster built by teenagers to guard over Plants Brook Local Nature Reserve in Birmingham.

Nature clubs and holiday play-schemes help involve local children and their families. Examples of the type of activities that might be appropriate include making animal masks, wildflower painting, adventure walks and bird spotting.

LOOK OUT & ABOUT *at*

BUCKPOOL & FENS POOL
NATURE RESERVE

Look Out and About

THE MOORHEN

T h e Moorhen has dark plumage with white patches showing on its flanks and under its tail which it often flicks.
It has a red bill with a yellow tip. It is more nervous than the Coot and is usually seen swimming along the edge of the water.

What colour legs has the Moorhen?

Answer:...................................Score | 10 |

Date Seen:...............................Score | 5 |

Look Out and About

THE FOX

Foxes come out mainly at night to search for their food. They eat all sorts of things including worms and will even look in your dustbin fo scraps to eat.
Do you know what the tail of a fox is calle

Answer:...............................Score

Date Seen:...........................Score

Look Out and About

YOU AND YOUR SCORES

It will be a big day for you when you reach your 400 — or even your 300 — points!
So when you have as many points as you can get, ask your teacher or parent to check the entries in the book and if they are satisfied that it is all your own work, they should sign on the opposite page.
After filling in your name and address, and the name of your school, send the book to the Warden at the address shown opposite and we will have a look at it.
When all your points have been counted up, the book will be returned to you with a **Nature Detective Certificate** and a **LOOK OUT and ABOUT** lapel badge.
For those of you who do really well, there will also be a prize.

So go out NOW, and collect as many points as you can!

Good Luck.

Figure 7.5   Pages from the Pensnett Wildlife Group's booklet

114

7.4 Evaluating and improving the use and management of a site

After an event has been held, signs and panels have been produced or a project has been completed, it is important to take stock, record what has been done, and assess the outcome. Which activities have been most popular, worthwhile and enjoyable? Are the signs effective? Has the project been successful? This information will help others who might be involved in managing, promoting and interpreting the site in future, as well as providing guidance for further improvements. Each event provides the opportunity to ask people what should be done next to encourage them to remain involved. Suggestion boxes and simple optional questionnaires can be used to provide additional feedback.

Over time, the nature of the site and the local community are likely to change, so that there will be a continuing need to reassess and update your plans for promotion and interpretation, as well as for site management. As the years pass, you should have the great satisfaction of seeing your efforts rewarded not only in the benefits for wildlife but also in an increasing appreciation of the value of urban wildlife areas among all members of the community.

FURTHER READING

The following list includes books that were used as source material and that we would recommend as further reading. The first three books cover a variety of topics. The other books are listed under their main topic.

Chinery, M, Teagle, W G (1985) *Wildlife in Towns and Cities – Gardens, Parks and Waterways*. Feltham, Middlesex, Hamlyn

Emery, M (1986) *Promoting Nature in Cities and Towns – A Practical Guide*. Croom Helm, London

London Ecology Unit (1990) *Nature Areas for City People – Ecology Handbook 14*. London, London Ecology Unit

Campaigning

King, A, Clifford, S (1985) *Holding Your Ground – An Action Guide to Local Conservation*. London, Maurice Temple Smith

Grants and advice

Charities Aid Foundation (1991) *Directory of Grant-Making Trusts*. Tonbridge, Charities Aid Foundation (updated every two years)

Shell Better Britain Campaign (1992) *Getting Help for Community Environmental Projects*. Birmingham, Shell Better Britain Campaign (separate versions available for England, Northern Ireland, Scotland and Wales)

Habitat creation

Baines, C, Smart, J (1991) *A Guide to Habitat Creation*. London, London Ecology Unit

Interpretation and promotion

English Nature (1984 onwards) *Urban Wildlife News*. Peterborough, English Nature (quarterly newsletter, providing national and international coverage of nature conservation events and activities in urban areas)

Millward, A, Mostyn, B (1989) *People and Nature in Cities*. Peterborough, Nature Conservancy Council

Management specifications

Leicester City Council (1990) *Open Space Management for Nature Conservation – Introducing Nature Conservation into Local Authority Grounds Maintenance through Competitive Tendering*. Leicester, Leicester City Council

Schools and wildlife

Learning through Landscapes Trust (1990) *Using School Grounds as an Educational Resource*. Winchester, Learning through Landscapes Trust

Smith, D (1984) *Urban Ecology*. London, Allen and Unwin (suggestions for projects, mainly at sixth-form level)

Soils

Bullock, P, Gregory, P J (eds) (1991) *Soils in the Urban Environment*. Oxford, Blackwell Scientific Publications

Hollis, J M (1992) *Proposals for the Classification, Description and Mapping of Soils in Urban Areas*. Peterborough, English Nature

Urban ecology

Barker, G, Graf, A (1989) *Principles for Nature Conservation in Towns and Cities. Urban Wildlife Now Number 3*. Peterborough, Nature Conservancy Council

Bornkamm, R, Lee, J A, Seaward, M R D (eds) (1982) *Urban Ecology – 2nd European Ecological Symposium*. London, Blackwell Scientific

Gilbert, O L (1991) *The Ecology of Urban Habitats*. London, Chapman and Hall

Sukopp, H, Werner, P (1982) *Nature in Cities – Nature and Environment Series No. 28*. Strasbourg, Council in Europe

Sukopp, H, Werner, P (1987) *Development of Flora and Fauna in Urban Areas – Nature and Environment Series No. 36*. Strasbourg, Council of Europe

Urban habitats

Ash, H J, Bennett, R, Scott, R (1992) *Flowers in the Grass*. Peterborough, English Nature

Flint, R (1985) *Encouraging Wildlife in Urban Parks – Guidelines to Management*. London, The London Wildlife Trust

Gemmell, R P (1982) The origin and botanical importance of industrial habitats. In: *Urban Ecology*, pp. 33–39. Bornkamm, R, Lee, J A, Seaward, M R D (eds) *Urban Ecology*, pp. 33–39

Gilbert, O (1992) *Rooted in Stone – The Natural Flora of Urban Walls*. Peterborough, English Nature

Gilbert, O (1992) *The Flowering of the Cities – The Natural Flora of Urban Commons*. Peterborough, English Nature

Gilbert, O L, Pearman, M C (1988) Wild figs by the Don. In: *Sheffield's Urban Wildlife*, pp. 31–33. Whiteley, D (ed). Sheffield, Sorby Natural History Society in collaboration with the Nature Conservancy Council

Teagle, W G (1978) *The Endless Village* (2nd edition). Shrewsbury, Nature Conservancy Council

Urban wildlife habitat surveys

Cardiff Wildlife Group (1984) Cardiff Wildlife Survey (unpublished)

Dawson, D, Game, M (1987) Biological Survey for Nature Conservation Planning. London, London Ecology Unit (unpublished)

Dawson, D, Game, M (1988) Habitat Survey for Greater London (unpublished)

Nature Conservancy Council (1990) *Handbook for Phase I Habitat Survey A Technique for Environmental Audit*. Peterborough, Nature Conservancy Council

Nature Conservancy Council, City of Dundee District Council and Dundee Urban Wildlife Project (1988) Dundee Urban Wildlife Project – An Assessment of the City's Green Spaces (unpublished)

Wild, M, Gilbert, O (eds) (1988) Sheffield Inner City Habitat Survey (unpublished)

Urban wildlife sites

London Ecology Unit (1988) *Nature Conservation in Hillingdon – Ecology Handbook 7*. London, London Ecology Unit

London Ecology Unit (1989) *Nature Conservation in Southwark – Ecology Handbook 12*. London, London Ecology Unit (similar booklets for many other London boroughs have been published)

Phillips, S, Slade, S (1989) *The Green in the Grey*. London, PNL Press

Smyth, B (1987) *City Wildspace*. London, Shipman

Wildlife and planning policy

Countryside Commission (1987) *Planning for Countryside in Metropolitan Areas – Guidance for the Preparation of Unitary Development Plans*. Cheltenham, Countryside Commission

Countryside Commission (1991) *Green Capital – Planning for London's Greenspace*. Cheltenham, Countryside Commission

Leicester City Council (1989) *Leicester Ecology Strategy*. Leicester, Leicester City Council

Nature Conservancy Council (1987) *Planning for Wildlife in Metropolitan Areas*. Peterborough, Nature Conservancy Council

Nature Conservancy Council (1988) *Tyne and Wear Nature Conservation Strategy*. Peterborough, Nature Conservancy Council

Simmons, S A, Pocock, R L and Barker, A (1990) *Nature Conservation in Towns and Cities: A Framework for Action*. Peterborough, Nature Conservancy Council

The Greater London Council (1984) *Ecology and Nature Conservation in London – Ecology Handbook No. 1*. London, London Ecology Unit

The Greater London Council (1985) *Nature Conservation Guidelines for London – Ecology Handbook No. 3*. London, London Ecology Unit

Appendix II
GLOSSARY

Annual A plant that completes its life cycle, from seed germination to seed production followed by death, within a single season.

Area of Deficiency A planning designation used by some local authorities to define urban areas where there are no sites of wildlife interest, with at least some public access, within 'easy reach' (in London, guidelines issued by the former Greater London Council defined 'easy reach' as within 1 kilometre of a Site of Metropolitan or Borough Importance).

Area of Special Character A designation used by some London boroughs to safeguard the individual quality and character of areas of open land and their architectural and historic features, with an emphasis on protecting the character of the skyline and exploiting recreational possibilities.

Arthropod An *invertebrate* animal with segmented body and jointed legs, such as insects, spiders, centipedes, millipedes and crustaceans.

Berm A shelf or ledge in the bank of a watercourse or water body.

Biennial A plant that requires two years to complete its life cycle from seed germination to seed production and death.

Calcicole A plant that thrives on calcareous or alkaline soils, such as those on chalk or limestone (and, in urban areas, alkaline wastes).

Canopy In woodland, the uppermost layer of foliage, formed by the crowns of trees.

Climax community The end point of an undisturbed succession under the prevailing climatic and soil conditions.

Compulsory competitive tendering (CCT) A requirement under the Local Government Act 1988 for local authorities to put many key services out to tender, including grounds maintenance.

Coppicing Felling trees close to the ground every few years, producing regular crops of young shoots for poles and firewood.

Coupe A coppice plot cut on a regular basis, usually in rotation with other coupes.

Detailed planning permission Gives permission for change of land use; work must commence within 5 years of approval if the permission is not to lapse.

Ecology strategy See *Nature conservation strategy*.

Emergent aquatic plants Plants that grow in shallow water, rooting in the bottom mud but with part of the plant emerging out of the water.

Encapsulated countryside Remnant of rural landscape that has become surrounded by urban development.

Eutrophication A process whereby water becomes laden with organic and mineral nutrients, which can result in excessive algal growth.

Extra heavy standard A nursery-grown tree, more than 3.5 metres tall.

Gabion A basket, usually made of galvanised wire (traditionally of wicker), filled with stones, crushed concrete or earth and used for reinforcing the bank of a watercourse or water body.

Green belt A planning designation applied to irregular belts of rural land around some built-up areas; originally designed to control the spread of major cities such as London and Birmingham, to keep nearby settlements as distinct entities and to preserve a rural landscape, by limiting development in the belt to specific land uses.

Green plan See *Nature conservation strategy*.

High forest A forest consisting of trees that have been allowed to reach their full height and form a high closed canopy.

Host plant A plant that is required by another organism, such as an insect, in order for that organism to survive (some organisms rely on a single species of host plant, whereas others use a range).

Introduced species Species that have arrived in this country relatively recently, that is, within the time of recorded history. Long-established species of plants tend to have a richer community of animals dependent on them than species that have been more recently introduced, although this is by no means a universal rule.

Invertebrate   An animal without a backbone.

Layering   Practice of bringing part of a shoot into contact with soil to encourage it to take root and form a new plant at that point. (The term is sometimes used to mean laying.)

Laying   Management of a hedge by cutting part-way through the stems of trees and shrubs and bending the cut stems sideways to form a barrier (also known as *layering*, pleaching and plashing).

Legume   A member of the plant family Leguminosae, characterised by the fruit which is a bivalved pod.

Licence   In relation to land tenure, a form of tenure that allows limited rights to the use of a site but not exclusive possession; licences are always restricted to a stated time, have a stated limited purpose and cannot be sold to other people or sub-licensed.

Local Nature Reserve (LNR)   A statutory designation, under the National Parks and Access to the Countryside Act 1949, which local authorities can apply to land that they own or control; allows local authorities to create bylaws to prohibit activities that may damage the area.

Local plan   See *Structure plan*.

Melanism   Presence of increased concentrations of the dark brown pigment melanin.

Nature conservation strategy   A planning document used by some local authorities to spell out in detail their policies concerning the environment and nature conservation (may be titled an *ecology strategy*, a *green plan* or a variety of related names, depending on the local authority) .

Notch planting   A planting technique whereby tree roots are inserted into a conical hole made by a dibber or a 'T', 'H' or 'L' shaped slit made with a spade. Unsuitable for large trees or wet ground.

Nurse crop   A crop grown to encourage the growth of another crop, for example by providing protection from strongly competitive species or adverse weather conditions.

Outline planning permission   Gives permission in principle for a change of land use, but the developer must submit detailed proposals within 3 years if the permission is not to lapse.

Parcel   In relation to wildlife habitat surveys, an area characterised as a particular habitat type, as defined by the plant community or structure.

Peppercorn rent   A nominal, or token, rent.

Perennial   A plant that continues its growth from year to year.

pH   A measure of acidity and alkalinity on a scale from 0 to 14; pH 7 is neutral, less than 7 is acid and more than 7 is alkaline. In soils, a pH of 4.5 and below is regarded as extremely acid, pH 6.6–7.3 as neutral and a pH over 9 as strongly alkaline.

Phase I survey   In relation to wildlife habitat surveys, a relatively rapid survey to map and record the extent of the vegetation and wildlife habitat over a large area. In *Phase II*, the vegetation of selected areas is surveyed more precisely, and in *Phase III* management plans are drawn up for individual sites.

Pollarding   The practice of cutting the trunk of a tree at some distance from the ground (generally 3–4 metres) to encourage a crop of young shoots.

Puddled clay   Traditional lining material for ponds and canals, made by pounding clay and water to a dense mass that is resistant to water penetration.

Ruderal   An early coloniser of disturbed or waste ground.

Scarifying   Scratching the surface of a seed or the soil to encourage seed germination.

Seed bank   The accumulation of viable seeds in the soil, which are likely to germinate if the soil is disturbed.

Seed rain   Seeds that arrive at a site from elsewhere, for example blown in by the wind or carried by birds.

Site of Importance for Nature Conservation (SINC)
A planning designation used by the West Midlands County Council for their most important wildlife sites, identified with the help of the former Nature Conservancy Council. Originally there were three grades of SINC: Grade A of county importance, Grade B of borough importance, and Grade C of local importance. Grading has now been discontinued, since it was felt to encourage undervaluing of some sites.

Site of Special Scientific Interest (SSSI)   Statutory designation, under the Wildlife and Countryside Act 1981, applied by English Nature, the Countryside Council for Wales and Scottish Natural Heritage to an area because of the special interest of its flora, fauna, geology or physical geography.

Slot seeder A machine that cuts a slot in the ground, creating an opening in any existing vegetation, into which it plants the seeds.

Stratification The practice of exposing seed to moist cool conditions for a period of time to break seed dormancy.

Structure plan A plan that must be prepared by a county council, setting out a broad policy framework for land use and development in the county. Each district council must prepare a more detailed *local plan*, with a map of proposals, indicating the areas earmarked for particular uses and developments. In London boroughs and metropolitan districts, unitary development plans now combine the function of structure and local plans.

Sucker A shoot growing directly from the underground stem of a plant, often appearing at some distance from the parent plant.

Transect A line or belt of vegetation, selected as a sample for recording the species present in an area, or for studying changes in the composition of species over time.

Transplant A small tree, less than 1.2 metres tall, that has been moved one or more times in nursery beds to improve root development.

Tree Preservation Order (*TPO*) A statutory order that a local authority can place on a tree, a group of trees or woodland to help conserve the amenity of an area.

Understorey In woodland, the plant layer below the tree canopy.

Whip A young tree with a single slender stem, larger than a *transplant* but smaller than a *standard* tree (definition of height range varies with supplier, but generally refers to plants between 1.2 and 2.5 metres tall).

Wildlife Heritage Site A planning designation applied by local authorities in Berkshire to the areas they consider to be of great wildlife interest.

SCIENTIFIC NAMES FOR WILDLIFE SPECIES

Plants

Alexanders *Smyrnium olusatrum*

Alder *Alnus glutinosa*

Alpine lady's mantle *Alchemilla vestita*

Amphibious bistort *Polygonum amphibium*

Apple,
>Domesticated *Malus domestica*
>
>Crab *Malus sylvestris*

Ash *Fraxinus excelsior*

Australian swamp stonecrop *Crassula helmsii*

Azaleas Family Rhododendroideae

Bamboos Family Bambuseae

Beech *Fagus sylvatica*

Bent grasses *Agrostis* spp

Bilberry *Vaccinium myrtillus*

Birch,
>Hairy *Betula pubescens*
>
>Silver *Betula pendula*

Bird cherry   (*see* Cherry, bird)

Birdsfoot trefoil *Lotus corniculatus*

Black knapweed *Centaurea nigra*

Black medick *Medicago lupulina*

Black poplar (*see* Poplar, black)

Blackthorn   *Prunus spinosa*

Bluebell *Hyacinthoides non-scripta*

Bogbean   *Menyanthes trifoliata*

Boston ivy   *Parthenocissus tricuspidata*

Bramble *Rubus fruticosus*

Broad-leaved dock *Rumex obtusifolius*

Brooklime *Veronica beccabunga*

Broom *Cytisus scoparius*

Buddleia *Buddleia davidii*

Bulbous buttercup *Ranunculus bulbosus*

Burnet rose   (*see* Rose)

Bur-reed,
>Branched *Sparganium erectum*
>
>Unbranched *Sparganium emersum*

Buttercups *Ranunculus* spp

Cabbage,
>Bastard *Rapistrum rugosum*
>
>Warty *Bunias orientalis*

Camellia *Camellia* sp

Campion,
>Bladder *Silene vulgaris*
>
>White *Silene alba*

Canadian pondweed (*see* Pondweed)

Carnation-grass (Glaucous sedge) *Carex flacca*

Catsear *Hypochaeris radicata*

Centaury *Centaurium erythraea*

Cherry,
>Bird   *Prunus padus*
>
>Gean *Prunus avium*

Chewings fescue *Festuca rubra* ssp *commutata*

Chinese lantern *Physalis alkekengii*

Chinese mother of thousands *Saxifraga stolonifera*

Cleavers (*see* Goosegrass)

Clovers *Trifolium* spp

Clubmosses Family Lycopodiaceae

Clustered bellflower *Campanula glomerata*

Coltsfoot *Tussilago farfara*

Columbines *Aquilegia* spp

Comfrey *Symphytum officinale*

Common agrimony *Agrimonia eupatoria*

Common bent grass *Agrostis tenuis*

Common butterwort *Pinguicula vulgaris*

Common nettle   *Urtica dioica*

Common oak   (*see* Oak)

Common reed *Phragmites australis*

Common rockrose *Helianthemum nummularium*

Common sallow *Salix atrocinerea*

Common sedge *Carex nigra*

Common spike-rush *Eleocharis palustris*

Common spotted orchid *Dactylorhiza fuchsii*

Common storksbill *Erodium cicutarium*

Common water crowfoot *Ranunculus aquatalis*

Cow parsley *Anthriscus sylvestris*

Cowslip *Primula veris*

Cranesbills   *Geranium* spp

Creeping bent *Agrostis stolonifera*

Creeping buttercup *Ranunculus repens*

Creeping thistle *Cirsium arvense*

Crested dogstail *Cynosurus cristatus*

Crucifers Family Cruciferae

Cuckoo-pint *Arum maculatum*

Daffodil *Narcissus pseudonarcissus* cultivars

Daisy *Bellis perennis*

Dandelion *Taraxacum officinale*

Docks *Rumex* spp

Dogwood   *Cornus sanguinea*

Duckweeds *Lemna* spp

Dwarf creeping fescue *Festuca rubra* ssp *litoralis*

Dyer's rocket (Weld) *Reseda luteola*

Elder *Sambucus nigra*

Elms *Ulmus* spp

Everlasting peas *Lathyrus* spp

False oat-grass *Arrhenatherum elatius*

Ferns Order Filicopsida

Fescue grasses *Festuca* spp

Field angelica *Angelica sylvestris*

Field maple *Acer campestre*

Fig *Ficus carica*

Fir *Abies* spp

Flowering rush *Butomus umbellatus*

Fox-tail barley *Hordeum jubatum*

Garden mints *Mentha* spp

Globe flower *Trollius europaeus*

Golden rod *Solidago canadensis*

Goosegrass *Galium aparine*

Great burnet *Sanguisorba officinalis*

Greater celandine *Chelidonium majus*

Great reedmace (*see* Reedmace)

Ground elder *Aegopodium podagraria*

Guelder rose (*see* Rose)

Gypsy-wort *Lycopus europaeus*

Harebell *Campanula rotundifolia*

Hawkbits *Leontodon* spp

Hawthorn,

    Common *Crataegus monogyna*

    Midland *Crataegus laevigata*

    Ornamental *Crataegus* spp and cultivars

Hazel *Corylus avellana*

Heath grass *Nardus stricta*

Heather (Ling) *Calluna vulgaris*

Hedge woundwort *Stachys sylvatica*

Himalayan roses *Rosa* spp

Holly *Ilex aquifolium*

Honeysuckle *Lonicera periclymenum*

Hornbeam *Carpinus betulus*

Horse radish *Armoracia rusticana*

Horseshoe vetch *Hippocrepis comosa*

Horsetails *Equisetum* spp

Hybrid black poplar (*see* Poplar, black)

Irises *Iris* spp

Ivy *Hedera helix*

Japanese bleeding heart *Dicentra spectabilis*

Japanese knotweed *Reynoutria japonica*

Jasmine *Jasminium* spp

Kidney vetch *Anthyllis vulneraria*

Laburnum *Laburnum anagyroides*

Lady's bedstraw *Galium verum*

Lady's mantle (*see* Alpine lady's mantle)

Large campanula *Campanula latifolia*

Large-leaved lime (*see* Lime)

Laurel (Common or Cherry) *Prunus laurocerasus*

Lesser reedmace (*see* Reedmace)

Lesser spearwort *Ranunculus flammula*

Lime,

    Large-leaved *Tilia platyphyllos*

    Small-leaved *Tilia cordata*

London plane *Platanus × acerifolia*

Maples *Acer* spp

Marsh foxtail *Alopecurus geniculatus*

Marsh marigold *Caltha palustris*

Mat-grass *Nardus stricta*

Meadow buttercup *Ranunculus acris*

Meadow saxifrage *Saxifraga granulata*

Meadow-grasses *Poa* spp

Meadowsweet *Filipendula ulmaria*

Melilots *Melilotus* spp

Michaelmas daisy *Aster novi-belgii*

Millet,

    Common *Panicum miliaceum*

    Italian *Setaria italica*

Mint,

    Corn *Mentha arvensis*

    Water *Mentha aquatica*

Mountain ash (*see* Rowan)

Mountain peony *Paeonia suffruticosa*

Mudwort *Limosella aquatica*

Musk mallow *Malva moschata*

Oak,

    Pedunculate (Common) *Quercus robur*

    Sessile *Quercus petraea*

    Turkey *Quercus cerris*

Old man's beard *Clematis vitalba*

Orchids Family Orchidaceae

Osier, Common (*see* Willow)

Ox-eye daisy *Leucanthemum vulgare*

Oxford ragwort *Senecio squalidus*

Pansy,

    Field *Viola arvensis*
    Mountain *Viola lutea*

Pedunculate oak (*see* Oak)

Periwinkle (Lesser periwinkle) *Vinca minor*

Pignut *Conopodium majus*

Pines *Pinus* spp

Pirri-pirri bur *Acaena novaezelandica*

Plane (*see* London plane)

Plantain,
    Hoary *Plantago media*
    Ribwort   *Plantago lanceolata*
    Water *Alisma plantago-aquatica*
Pondweed,
    Broad-leaved *Potamogeton natans*
    Canadian *Elodea canadensis*
    Curled   *Potamogeton crispus*
    Fennel *Potamogeton pectinatus*
    Perfoliate *Potamogeton perfoliatus*
    Various-leaved *Potamogeton gramineus*
Poplar,
    Black *Populus nigra*
    Manchester *Populus nigra var. betulifolia*
    White *Populus alba*
Poppy,
    Field *Papaver rhoeas*
    Long-headed *Papaver dubium*
Privet,
    Garden *Ligustrum ovalifolium*
    Wild   *Ligustrum vulgare*
Purging flax *Linum catharticum*
Pyracanthas *Pyracantha* spp
Quaking grass *Briza media*
Ragged robin *Lychnis flos-cuculi*
Ragwort (*see* Oxford ragwort)
Red hot poker *Kniphofia* spp
Red rattle   *Odontites verna*
Reed canary grass *Phalaris arundinacea*
Reed sweet-grass *Glyceria maxima*
Reedmace,
    Great (Bulrush) *Typha latifolia*
    Lesser *Typha angustifolia*
Reflexed salt-marsh-grass *Puccinellia distans*
Rhododendron *Rhododendron* spp
Rose,
    Burnet *Rosa pimpinellifolia*
    Dog   *Rosa canina*
    Guelder *Viburnum opulus*

Rosebay willowherb *Chamaenerion angustifolium*
Rough hawkbit *Leontodon hispidus*
Rowan (Mountain ash) *Sorbus aucuparia*
Rushes *Juncus* spp
Russian vine *Fallopia aubertii*
Rye-grasses *Lolium* spp
Sainfoin *Onobrychis viciifolia*
Salad burnet *Sanguisorba minor*
Saxifrage,
    Burnet *Pimpinella saxifraga*
    Greater burnet *Pimpinella major*
    Pepper *Silaum silaus*
Scabious,
    Devil's-bit *Succisa pratensis*
    Small *Scabiosa columbaria*
Scarlet pimpernel   *Anagallis arvensis*
Sedges *Carex* spp
Self-heal *Prunella vulgaris*
Sessile oak   (*see* Oak)
Sheep's sorrel   *Rumex acetosella*
Shepherd's purse *Capsella bursa-pastoris*
Small balsam *Impatiens parviflora*
Small toadflax *Chaenorrhinum minus*
Small-leaved lime   (*see* Lime)
Smooth sedge *Carex laevigata*
Smooth-stalked meadow-grass *Poa pratensis*
Soapwort   *Saponaria officinalis*
Sorrel *Rumex acetosa*
Spiked water-milfoil *Myriophyllum spicatum*
Spotted dead-nettle *Lamium maculatum*
Spruces *Picea* spp
Stonecrop *Sedum* sp
Storksbills *Geranium* spp

Sunflower   *Helianthus annuus*
Sweet chestnut *Castanea sativa*
Sweet cicely *Myrrhis odorata*
Sweet flag   *Acorus calamus*
Sycamore   *Acer pseudoplatanus*
Tansy *Chrysanthemum vulgare*
Thistles *Cirsium* spp
Trefoils *Lotus* spp
Turkey oak   (*see* Oak)
Upright hedge-parsley *Torilis japonica*
Vervain *Verbena officinalis*
Vetches *Vicia* spp
Vetchlings *Lathyrus* spp
Violet,
    Common *Viola riviniana*
    Hairy *Viola hirta*
    Marsh *Viola palustris*
Virginia creeper *Parthenocissus quinquefolia*
Water fern   *Azolla filiculoides*
Water forget-me-not *Myosotis scorpioides*
Water horsetail *Equisetum fluviatile*
Water lily,
    Fringed *Nymphoides peltata*
    White *Nymphaea alba*
    Yellow *Nuphar lutea*
Watercress   *Nasturtium officinale*
Wayfaring tree *Viburnum lantana*
Westerwolds rye-grass *Lolium multiflorum*
White clover *Trifolium repens*
Whitebeam,
    Common *Sorbus aria*
    Swedish *Sorbus intermedia*
Wild carrot *Daucus carota*
Willow,
    Crack *Salix fragilis*
    Dwarf *Salix herbacea*
    Eared *Salix aurita*
    Goat *Salix caprea*
    Osier *Salix viminalis*
    White *Salix alba*

Willows *Salix* spp
Wisteria *Wisteria* spp
Wood anemone *Anemone nemorosa*
Woody nightshade *Solanum dulcamara*
Yarrow *Achillea millefolium*
Yellow archangel *Lamiastrum galeobdolon*
Yellow flag *Iris pseudacorus*
Yellow rattle *Rhinanthus minor*
Yorkshire fog *Holcus lanatus*

Animals

Beetles Order Coleoptera
Black redstart *Phoenicurus ochruros*
Blackbird *Turdus merula*
Caddis flies Order Trichoptera
Coot *Fulica atra*
Crow (Carrion) *Corvus corone corone*

Damselflies Order Odonata – Suborder Zygoptera
Dragonflies Order Odonata – Suborder Anisoptera
Feral pigeon (Feral rock dove) *Columba livia*
Finches Family Fringillidae
Fox *Vulpes vulpes*
Frog *Rana temporaria*
Great crested grebe *Podiceps cristatus*
Great crested newt *Triturus cristatus*
Great northern diver *Gavia immer*
Grey dagger *Acronicta psi*
Grey squirrel *Squirus carolinensis*
Hedgehog *Erinaceus europaeus*
Herring gull *Larus argentatus*
House sparrow *Passer domesticus*
Hoverflies Order Diptera – Family Syrphidae

Jackdaw *Corvus monedula*
Jay *Garrulus glandarius*
Kestrel *Falco tinnunculus*
Magpie *Pica pica*
Mayflies Order Ephemeroptera
Mottled beauty *Cleora repandata*
Muntjac deer *Muntiacus reevesi*
Newts *Triturus* spp
Pale brindled beauty *Apocheima pilosaria*
Peppered moth *Biston betularia*
Pipistrelle bat *Pipistrellus pipistrellus*
Rabbit *Oryctolagus cuniculus*
Scalloped hazel *Odontoptera bidentata*
Short-tailed vole *Microtus agrestis*
Starling *Sturnus vulgaris*
Stoneflies Order Plecoptera
Waved umber *Menophra abruptaria*
Weasel *Mustela nivalis*

Acknowledgements

The Open University Course Team is greatly indebted to the many people, with a wide range of experience of urban wildlife and wildlife site management, who have contributed to the development of this teaching programme.

First, we must acknowledge the very generous financial support of English Nature, the Esmée Fairbairn Charitable Trust and the Ernest Cook Trust.

We also value the comments and the support of the external assessor, Professor B Green, The Sir Cyril Kleinwort Professor of Countryside Management, Wye College, University of London.

We would also like to thank all those who have provided source material for the book or read and commented on preliminary drafts:

George Barker (English Nature)
Gareth Barton (Pensnett Wildlife Group)
Christine Blackmore (Open University)
John Box (English Nature)
Julie Brownbridge (London Ecology Unit)
Roger Butterfield (Sheffield City Wildlife Trust)
Linda Carter (Reading Urban Wildlife Group)
Richard Clarke (London University)
Oliver Gilbert (Sheffield University)

Monica Hale (BES/CEE, University of Reading)
Helen Hall (Avon Wildlife Trust)
Ted Hammond (English Nature)
Andrew Jones (Scottish Conservation Projects)
Antony Merritt (Avon Wildlife Trust)
Alison Silk (City of Dundee District Council)
Judy Ling Wong (Black Environment Network)
Mary Young (Friends of Forest Lane Park).

Index